MW00768649

ROBIN NIXON'S
JAVASCRIPT
CRASH COURSE

Learn JavaScript in 14 easy lectures

ROBIN NIXON'S
JAVASCRIPT
CRASH COURSE

Learn JavaScript in 14 easy lectures

Robin Nixon

Nixon
Publishing

ROBIN NIXON'S JAVASCRIPT CRASH COURSE

By Robin Nixon

Copyright © 2012/13 Nixon Publishing, 4 Coast Drive, New Romney, Kent TN28 8NX, UK

Published by: Nixon Publishing
                4 Coast Drive
                Greatstone
                New Romney
                Kent TN28 8NX
                United Kingdom

Email: info@nixonpublishing.com
Website: nixonpublishing.com

The publisher, the author and anyone else involved in preparing this work make no representations or warrantees with respect to the accuracy or completeness of the contents of this work, and specifically disclaim all warrantees, including without limitation any implied warrantees of fitness for a particular purpose.

Any Internet web addresses linked to other than our own may change during the lifetime of this publication and readers should be prepared to use a search engine such as Google to locate alternative websites should this happen.

Many web addresses (URLs) have been shortened using the *tinyurl.com* shortening service to make them easier for you to enter.

No warrantee may be created or extended by any promotional statements made for this work. Neither the publisher nor the author shall be liable for any damages arising herefrom.

All the examples files from this course are in a file named *examples.zip*, which you can download at *tinyurl.com/jsccexamples*. Each lecture has an associated folder in this archive named *Lecture 1* through *Lecture 14*, in which the examples for each matching lecture can be found.

ISBN: 978-0-9568956-3-9

For Julie

About the author

Robin Nixon has been a writer for 30 years, has written in excess of 500 articles for many of the UK's top magazines, and has authored over a dozen books.

Robin started his writing career in the Cheshire homes for disabled people, where he was responsible for setting up computer rooms in a number of residential homes, evaluating and tailoring hardware and software so that disabled people could use the new technology, and writing supporting documentation and articles for a selection of national magazines. After this Robin's career became a hundred percent writing-oriented when he joined a large magazine publisher, where he held a variety of different editorial positions, before leaving to become a self-employed writer.

With the dawn of the Internet in the 1990s, Robin branched out into developing websites (including the world's first licensed Internet radio station). In order to enable people to continue to surf while listening, Robin also developed the first known pop-up windows. In the late 1990s and early 2000s Robin and his family moved to the USA a couple of times, once to run a web design company in California, and then again to set up an English Tearoom in Texas. In between times they ran several successful pubs, bed and breakfasts and nightclubs in England.

In recent years Robin has begun to focus more closely on motivation and personal improvement in his writing, while still continuing to produce more in his popular series of books on computing, which have now been translated into several different languages. Robin lives on the south-east coast of England (where he writes full time), along with his five children and wife Julie (a trained nurse and university lecturer) – between them they also foster three disabled children.

Other books by Robin Nixon

- ➤ *Learning PHP, MySQL and JavaScript*, O'Reilly 2009
- ➤ *Plug-in PHP*, McGraw-Hill 2010
- ➤ *Plug-in JavaScript*, McGraw-Hill 2010
- ➤ *Plug-in CSS*, McGraw-Hill 2011
- ➤ *HTML5 For iOS And Android*, McGraw-Hill, 2011
- ➤ *Robin Nixon's CSS & CSS3 Crash Course*, Nixon, 2011
- ➤ *Robin Nixon's HTML & HTML5 Crash Course*, Nixon, 2011
- ➤ *Robin Nixon's JavaScript Crash Course*, Nixon, 2012
- ➤ *The Web Developer's Cookbook*, McGraw-Hill, 2012

TABLE OF CONTENTS

Lecture 8: Controlling Program Flow 105

Lecture 9: Looping Sections of Code 119

LEARN JAVASCRIPT THE QUICK AND EASY WAY

IF YOU KNOW HTML and/or CSS and want to take your skills to the next level, or even if you are a complete web novice, you really need to learn JavaScript. Not only is it the language behind the smooth and dynamic operation of Web 2.0 websites like Facebook, Twitter and Gmail, but in conjunction with HTML5 it's also the standard means Microsoft supports for creating Windows 8 apps - JavaScript is definitely the future for Windows!

So, whether you want to simply add a little functionality to your website, such as smooth menus that pop up and down, image transition effects, user-friendly form handling and verification, or anything else that's more than a simple, flat HTML/CSS design, JavaScript is the way to go.

What's more, JavaScript is easy. If you've ever tried to learn it and been put off by a plethora of jargon and technical mumbo-jumbo then you're in for a real treat, because Robin Nixon's Crash Courses have helped tens of thousands of people learn the new skills they need.

Starting from the ground up with no assumption of prior knowledge, every aspect of JavaScript is explained in this book, in logical order with plenty of simple examples, clear explanations, informative figures, and advice on how best to use the new things you learn.

If you want to learn JavaScript up to a solid intermediate level, this book will teach you all you need to know, without recourse to other books and materials. Plus all the examples are free to download from the companion website, so you won't have to type them in to follow along.

About This Course

This course is based on about 15 years' experience of programming in JavaScript and is written using the same easy-to-follow style as my best-selling book, *Learning PHP, MySQL and JavaScript*. In it I talk to you in plain English, explaining everything you need to know about each feature in a variety of different ways, using lots of example code, screen shots and tables, so that you will learn quickly and easily.

My intention is that you will learn to be a good JavaScript programmer in under 14 hours, by spending one hour or less on each lecture. At one lecture a day you'll become proficient in two weeks. Or if you have a free weekend, then it'll be a couple of days. And that's including starting from the very first principles such as learning what variables and operators are.

I have taught tens of thousands of people to program over the years and the main comment I receive is "You make it seem so easy", so I hope you will agree and this crash course will be all you need to take you to the next level in your web development.

The Example Files

To save you typing them in and to avoid introducing typographical errors, all the examples in this book can be downloaded from the companion website at the following URL. Just click on the *Download Examples* link to retrieve the *examples.zip* archive, which you can extract to obtain all the files, which are located by lecture into folders *Lecture 1* though *Lecture 14.*:

   javascriptcrashcourse.com

Thanks And Good Luck

Thanks again for purchasing this book. I hope you find it teaches you everything you want to know and helps you to the next level in your web development endeavors.

- Robin Nixon

INTRODUCTION TO JAVASCRIPT

By following this lecture you will:

✓ *Obtain an overview of what JavaScript is and how to use it.*

✓ *Learn the history of the JavaScript language.*

✓ *Be introduced to some of the features you'll be learning about.*

JAVASCRIPT IS THE free language built into all modern browsers including Internet Explorer, Firefox, Safari, Opera and Chrome. It is the power behind dynamic HTML and the Ajax environment used for Web 2.0 websites such as Facebook, Flickr, Gmail and many others.

This course is aimed squarely at people who have learned basic HTML (and perhaps a little CSS) but are interested in doing more. For example, you may wish to create more dynamic menu systems, provide mouse hover effects, support Ajax functionality and more. During this course you'll be shown how to do all these things and much more using JavaScript.

As you progress it is never assumed that you know anything about a solution, and you are taken through each example step by step with the explanations included, so there is no need to look up anything elsewhere. Note: All the examples files from this course are in a ZIP archive, which you can download at the following URL:

tinyurl.com/jsccexamples

A Little History

The JavaScript programming language was written by Brendan Eich at Netscape, and was previously known by both of the names Mocha and LiveScript. It was first incorporated into the Netscape Navigator browser in 1995, at the same time that Netscape added support for Sun's Java technology.

JavaScript is a quite different language from Java but, as part of a marketing deal made between Netscape and Sun Microsystems, it was given its name to try and benefit from the general buzz surrounding the Java language. To justify this naming, in JavaScript all Java keywords are reserved, its standard library follows Java's naming conventions, and its Math and Date objects are based on Java 1.0 classes, and the trademark name JavaScript also belongs to Sun—but the similarities end there.

Microsoft's version, called JScript, was released a year later as a component of Internet Explorer 3.0 and, as you might expect, it differed in several important respects, making it less than 100% compatible with JavaScript. Unfortunately that remains true to this day, although Internet Explorer 9 has addressed many of the prior incompatibilities, and IE10 looks set to become even more compatible with the other browsers.

Unlike other languages used for creating websites, such as Perl, PHP and Ruby, JavaScript runs within the web browser, and not on a web server. This makes it the perfect tool for creating dynamic web pages because it can modify HTML elements in real time. It is also the technology behind web 2.0 Ajax functionality, in which data is transferred between a web server and web browser behind the scenes, without the user being aware of it.

JavaScript's great power lies in its ability to access HTML's Document Object Model (DOM), in which every element on a web page can be individually addressed (either reading or modifying its value), and elements can also be created and deleted on the fly, as well as layered over each other and moved about. You can even go so far as to treat a web browser window as a blank canvas and build entire applications and arcade games from scratch using JavaScript and the DOM (although doing so takes some quite advanced programming skills).

Because Sun owns the trademark to its name, ever since the language was submitted to ECMA, the European Computer Manufacturers Association (a non-profit standards organization), JavaScript has officially been known as ECMAScript.

Info for Programmers

If you can already program in another language such as C or Java (for example) you'll find yourself at home with JavaScript, and here are a few things you should know about the language that will make your learning process even quicker. If you are not a programmer you may skip to the next section as these terms will be explained later in the course.

To begin with JavaScript supports much of the structured programming syntax used in C such as `if()` statements, `while()` and `for()` loops, `switch()` statements and so on. Unlike many languages it is not necessary to terminate statements with a semicolon, unless more statements will follow on the same line.

JavaScript is a scripting language and is not compiled, and in common with other scripting languages it uses dynamic typing in which types are associated with values rather than variables. Values are interpreted as integers, floating point, strings or other types according to the way in why they are used within an expression.

The JavaScript language is based on objects which are associative arrays. Properties of objects can be accessed using either the period operator (for example, `object.height`) or with square braces (for example, `object['height']`. Object properties can be enumerated using `for(… in …)` loops.

In JavaScript, functions are themselves objects, so they have properties such as length and methods such as `call()`. This means they may also be assigned to variables, passed as arguments and returned by other functions. Functions are referenced by naming them without a pair of round brackets (for example, `a = funcname`) or invoked by adding the brackets (for example, `a = funcname()`).

The former case sets the variable a to contain a copy of the function object with the name `funcname`, while the latter assigns the result returned by calling the function to the variable `a`. You may create inner functions within other functions, and these retain the scope of the outer function, including its constants, local variables and argument values.

Rather than implementing classes, JavaScript used prototypes for inheritance. Functions can double as object constructors, and prefixing a function with the `new` keyword creates a new object, calling that function with its local `this` keyword.

Summary

As I said, if you are new to programming, don't worry about any of these terms because I will explain them later in the course at the appropriate places. And I promise, they are just words, and their use will become second nature to you as you learn JavaScript, because it really is a simple language to learn.

INCORPORATING JAVASCRIPT CODE INTO A WEB PAGE

By following this lecture you will:

- ✓ *Learn how to use single and multi-line comments..*
- ✓ *Understand the purpose of semicolons.*
- ✓ *Know how to include JavaScript in your web pages.*

THE WHOLE POINT of JavaScript is that it is designed to offer dynamic functionality to what previously were static web pages. Therefore JavaScript code is generally embedded within a web page to which it applies. This can be in the form of the direct code itself, or by means of a tag that tells the browser the location of a file containing some JavaScript to load in and execute. This external file may be on the same or a different web server.

Additionally, the location within a web page at which you insert the JavaScript (or link to a JavaScript file) becomes the default location in which any output from the JavaScript will be inserted. Of course, being a programming language, you can tell it exactly where in a web page to display anything, but if you use a simple JavaScript function such as `write()`, it will insert whatever is written in the current location.

Therefore, for this and other reasons, where you place your JavaScript can be important, and I will explain how you can choose the right location a little later on. Firstly, though, let's take a look at the basics.

Using Comments

Before looking at the JavaScript language and its syntax, I want to introduce the commenting feature. Using comments you can add text to a JavaScript program that explains what it does. This will help you later when you are debugging, and is especially helpful when other people have to maintain code that you write.

There are two ways to create a comment in JavaScript, the first of which is to preface it with two slashes, as follows:

```
// This is a comment
```

You can place a comment after a JavaScript statement, like this:

```
anumber = 42 // Assigns 42 to anumber
```

Or, if you wish to temporarily restrict a line of code from executing, you can insert a comment tag before it and the statement will be completely ignored, like this:

```
// anumber = 42
```

Sometimes you need to be able to comment out more than a single line of text. In which case you can use the multi-line form of commenting in which you start the comment with /*, and end it with */, like this:

```
/* This is a multi-line
   set of comments, which
   can appear over any
   number of lines      */
```

Note: *As well as supporting extensive documentation, this form of commenting lets you temporarily comment out complete blocks of code by simply placing the start and end tags as required – something that can be extremely helpful when debugging.*

Using Semicolons

If you like you may add a semicolon after every JavaScript statement, and many programmers choose to do this. However, I prefer not to since semicolons are not mandatory. On the other hand, if you wish to place more than one statement on a single line then you must separate them with a semicolon. So, for example, the three following sets of code are all valid syntax:

```
a = 1
b = 2

a = 1; b = 2

a = 1;
b = 2;
```

However, the following is not valid, as JavaScript will not know how to make sense of it due to the omission of a semicolon:

```
a = 1 b = 2
```

Note: Think of the semicolon as acting line a new line as far as the JavaScript interpreter is concerned (or vice versa). If in doubt, always add one and, although you may end up with more semicolons than you need, at least your code will run correctly (assuming no other errors). In this course, however, I use semicolons only where they are necessary

Where to Place the JavaScript Code

As previously mentioned, it can make a difference where you place your JavaScript code. For example, if you wish default output to go straight into the current document, you may choose to place your JavaScript directly within the `<body>` and `</body>` tags. On the other hand, if you have a very long web page that takes more than a second or so to load, you might choose to place your JavaScript code within the `<head>` and `</head>` tags, so that it will be executed as soon as that part of the document is loaded in.

In the Document Head

To insert your JavaScript within the head of a document you must place `<script>` and `</script>` tags where the script is to go, like this (highlighted in bold text):

```
<html>
  <head>
    <title>Page Title</title>
    <script>
      // Your JavaScript goes here
    </script>
  </head>
  <body>
    The document body goes here
```

```
    </body>
  </html>
```

In the Document Body

To insert your JavaScript within the body of a document you must place `<script>` and `</script>` tags where the script is to go, like this (highlighted in bold text):

```
<html>
  <head>
    <title>Page Title</title>
  </head>
  <body>
    The document body goes here
    <script>
      // Your JavaScript goes here
    </script>
  </body>
</html>
```

Including JavaScript Files

If you wish to keep your JavaScript code separate from your document contents (something you are likely to want to do once your JavaScript starts to become any length other than small), you can place it in its own file (usually with the file extension *.js*) and, instead of inserting script between `<script>` and `</script>` tags, you would include the code like this (highlighted in bold text):

```
<html>
  <head>
    <title>Page Title</title>
    <script src='myscript.js'></script>
  </head>
  <body>
    The document body goes here
  </body>
</html>
```

If the script file is not in the current director you must include the path along with the filename, like this:

```
<script src='pathtofolder/myscript.js'></script>
```

Or if the code is on another server, include the correct `http://` (or `https://` prefix, domain and path) like this:

```
<script src='http://server.com/folder/script.js'></script>
```

When including a script rather than embedding it in a web document, you may still choose where you wish to insert it, for example into the body rather than the head, like this:

```
<html>
  <head>
    <title>Page Title</title>
  </head>
  <body>
    <script src='myscript.js'></script>
    The document body goes here
  </body>
</html>
```

Summary

Now that you know how and where to put JavaScript in your web pages, in the following lecture I'll begin to explain the syntax of the language.

JavaScript Language Syntax

By following this lecture you will:

- ✓ *Learn about case sensitivity.*
- ✓ *Understand the use of whitespace characters.*
- ✓ *Know how to use variables to store values.*

I'VE ALREADY DISCUSSED some of the *syntax* used by the JavaScript language, such as how to comment out sections of code, and where semicolons need to be used. But what is meant by syntax? Well, it's a set of rules that define how to correctly structure a JavaScript program.

In this section I'll outline the major syntax issues so that when you start programming you'll introduce the minimum of errors, so please forgive me if there's a little overlap with earlier sections.

Cases Sensitivity

JavaScript is what is known as a case-sensitive language. This means that it distinguishes between the use of the upper and lower case letters a-z and A-Z. So, for example, the variable MyVariable is quite different from myvariable (variables being special names used to stand in for values such as numbers or strings of characters, explained a little further on).

JavaScript will treat these as two totally different variables so you need to be careful when choosing your variable names. Generally I observe the following guidelines so that I can more easily go back and understand code I may have written some time in the past:

- All global variables that are accessible anywhere in a program are set to all uppercase, such as `HIGHSCORE`.
- Temporary variables used in loops are single letters in lower case, such as `j`.
- Function names use a capital letter at the start of each word, like this: `MyFunctionName()`.

This is only the formatting that I use, and you may choose to apply different upper and lower case rules to this, or simply stick to all lower case, it's entirely up to you.

Whitespace

Any spaces and tabs are known as whitespace, and any combination of these is usually treated by JavaScript as if it were a single space. The exception is when they are placed inside quotation marks, in which case they form part of a string, and all the characters are used.

Newline or carriage return characters are also treated as whitespace by JavaScript (unless within quotes), except that each one creates an implied semicolon which, as you saw in the previous section, is used to denote the end of a statement. Therefore, for example, the statement `a = b + c` is valid on a single line, but if you format it as follows, `a` will be assigned the value in `b`, and then an implied semicolon will be added, so that the `+ c` line following is then interpreted on its own, causing a syntax error:

```
a = b
+ c
```

Variables

A variable in any programming language is simply a container for a value. For example, imagine that you have a few empty plastic pots, into which you can place items (see Figure 3-1). Think of these as a metaphor for variables, in that you can take a small piece of paper and write the number `42` (for example) on it and insert it into one of the pots. If you then take a marker pen and write `MyVariable` on the pot, it is just like a JavaScript variable being set using this line of code:

```
MyVariable = 42
```

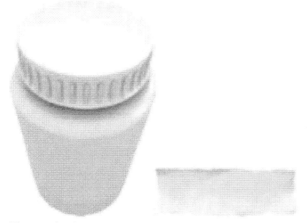

Figure 1: An empty pot and blank piece of paper.

Figure 3-2 shows the pot now labelled and the paper written on. You can now manipulate this variable in a variety of ways. For example, you can add another value to it, like this :

```
MyVariable = MyVariable + 13
```

This has the effect of adding `13` to the value of `42` already stored in the variable so that the result is `55`, the new value held in the variable. This is analogous to taking the piece of paper with the number `42` written on it out of the pot labelled `MyVariable`, noting the value, adding `13` to it, and then replacing that piece of paper with another on which you have written the number `55` (see Figure 3-3), which you then place back into the pot.

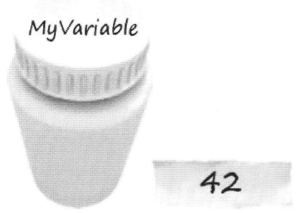

Figure 2: The pot has been labelled, and paper written on.

Figure 3: A new slip of paper with the number 55 on it.

Likewise you might issue the following command (for example), which will multiply the current value in the variable (55) by 3: `MyVariable = MyVariable * 3` Again, this is equivalent to taking the paper from the pot, performing the multiplication, and placing a new piece of paper with the result of `165` (see Figure 3-4) back into the pot.

All the time the current numeric value is updated and popped inside the pot with the label `MyVariable` on it, so that any time that value needs to be referenced (looked up), the pot can simply be opened and the slip of paper inside then read.

Variable Naming

There are a number of rules governing how you use the JavaScript programming language. For instance variables must begin with either an upper or lower case letter (`a-z` or `A-Z`), or the `$` or `_` symbols. No other character may begin a variable name.

Variables may not contain any mathematical operators (such as + or *), punctuation (such as ! or &), or spaces, but after the first character they may include the digits `0-9` or any of the characters that can begin a variable name. All JavaScript keywords (such as window, open, string, and so on) are reserved and may not be used as variable names.

String Variables

When a variable is used to store a number (as in the preceding examples) it's known as a numeric variable. However, it's also possible to store text in a variable, in which case the variable is called a string variable (since sequences of characters are called strings in programming languages).

Figure 4: Another piece of paper with the number 165 on it.

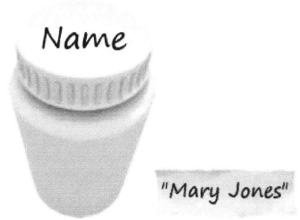

Figure 5: This pot is labelled "Name" and contains a string value.

Examples of strings include the name `"Bill Smith"`, the sequence of characters `"A23bQ%j"` and even the characters `"123"` which, in this case are a string of digits, not the number `123`.

In the same way that you can store a number in a variable, so you can a string, and you use the same method of assignment, like this:

```
Name = "Mary Jones"
```

Notice the use of double quotation marks around this string. These are what tell JavaScript that the value is a string, and is how you can assign the string `"123"` to a variable, as opposed to the number `123`, for example. In terms of the pot and paper metaphor, the preceding statement is equivalent to labelling a new pot as `"Name"` and writing `"Mary Jones"` on a piece of paper that you place in it, as shown in Figure 3-5.

Obviously you can't perform arithmetic on strings but there are other actions you can take such as shortening them, adding more characters to the front, middle or end, extracting a portion of a string value, and more. For example, you can concatenate two strings together (attach one to the other) using the same + operator you use for performing additions, like this:

```
Singer = "Paul"
Singer = Singer + " Simon"
```

The result of these two statements is to concatenate the string `"Paul"` (first assigned to, and then read from the variable `Singer`) with the string `" Simon"` and place the resulting string back into the variable `Singer`. In Lecture 6 I'll show you the other operations you can perform on strings.

Using Quotation Marks in Strings

You have seen the use of the double quote character to indicate the start and end of a string, but you may also use the single quote if you prefer, like this:

```
Dinner = 'Fish and Chips'
```

The end result is identical, whichever type of quotation marks you use.

But there is a good reason why you may choose one type instead of the other, and that's when you need to include a particular quotation mark within a string. For example, suppose you needed to store the string `"Isn't the weather fine?"`. As it stands, using double quotation marks works just fine, but what would happen if you surrounded the string with single quotation marks instead, like this: `'Isn't the weather fine?'`?

Well, you would get a syntax error because JavaScript would see only the string `'Isn'` and then some gibberish following it, like this: `t the weather fine?'`.

Then again what about the string `'Jane said, "Hello"'`? This time, using single quotes this string works, but because of the double quotes within it, if you were to surround the string with double quotes like this, `"Jane said, "Hello""`, JavaScript would see one string, like this: `"Jane said, "`, some gibberish (to JavaScript) like this: `Hello`, and another string with nothing in it, like this: `""`. It would give up at all this and generate an error.

Note: Placing a pair of quotes together with nothing between them results in what is called the empty string. It is commonly used for erasing or initializing the value of a string variable.

Escaping Characters

But things can get more interesting, because what about the occasions when you might require both types of quote to be included within a string, like this: `"Mark said, "I can't wait""`? As it stands this string will cause a syntax error, but you can easily fix it using the escape character, which is simply a backslash, like this: `"Mark said, \"I can't wait\""`.

What the escape character does is tell JavaScript to ignore the \ character and to use the character following it as a string element, and not a string container.

You may escape either of the quotation marks inside a string to ensure they are used only as string elements, and can also use escape characters to insert other characters that you cannot easily type in such as tabs and newlines, as follows:

- `\'` – single quote
- `\"` – double quote
- `\\` – backslash
- `\b` – backspace
- `\f` – form feed
- `\n` – new line
- `\r` – carriage return
- `\t` – tab

Variable Typing and Casting

In JavaScript, unlike some other programming languages, a variable can change its type automatically. For example a string can become a number, and vice versa, according to the way in which the variable is referenced. For example, take the following assignment in which the variable `MyVar` is given the string value of `"12345"`:

```
MyVar = "12345"
```

Although the string is created from a group of all digits, it is a string. However, JavaScript is smart enough to understand that sometimes a string can be a number, so in the following assignment it converts the string value in `MyVar` to a number prior to applying the subtraction, and then the resulting value (which is now the number `12000`) is stored back in `MyVar`, which is now a numeric variable:

```
MyVar = MyVar - 345
```

Likewise, a number can be automatically converted to a string, as in the following two lines, which first set the numeric variable `Time` to the value `6`, then the string

" O'clock" is appended to the number, which is first turned into a string to make this string concatenation possible:

```
Time = 6
Time = Time + " O'clock"
```

The result is that `Time` is now a string variable with the value `"6 O'clock"`.

Because of this changing of variables from one type to another (known as automatic type casting) it is not actually correct to think of JavaScript variables in terms of type, so I will no-longer do so. Instead you should consider only their contents and how JavaScript will interpret them.

However, sometimes it is necessary for you to force the type of a variable. For example, consider the following statement and ask yourself what you think JavaScript should do with it:

```
MyVar = "12345" + 678
```

If you think it will turn the string `"12345"` into a number and then add `678` to it (to result in the number `13023`) you are, unfortunately, wrong. Although that might seem the appropriate action, JavaScript chooses to turn the number `678` into the string `"678"` and then concatenate it with `"12345"`, resulting in the string `"12345678"`. If this is the result you want then that's good, but if not then you must force the type that JavaScript should use by using the function `Number()`, like this:

```
MyVar = Number("12345") + 678
```

Now, before you say, "Why not simply make the string a number in the first place?", consider the case of already having the variable `MyVar`, whose contents may be either a string or number (and you do not know which), but you then must add a number to it (rather than append a string) like this:

```
MyVar = MyVar + 678
```

If `MyVar` happens to be a string then a concatenation will occur, but if it is a number then an addition will take place. In this case it is therefore necessary to use the `Number()` function to ensure you always get the correct result intended, like this:

```
MyVar = Number(MyVar) + 678
```

Note: If you know for sure that you are only using numbers in a particular variable, and it will never contain anything else, then you will not need to use the Number() *function to cast the value. Generally the occasions on which you will find it beneficial to use casting are when dealing with values over which you have less control, such as user input that you are processing.*

The Cast Functions

There are three functions available for forcing the type of a variable (or casting it), as follows:

- Boolean() Cast the value to either true or false.
- Number() Cast the value to a number.
- String() Cast the value to a string.

Values that are cast to Boolean can become one of only two values: true or false. Any string of at least one character in length, any object, or any number greater than 0 will be cast to the value true. An empty string, the number 0, and the values undefined or null result in the value false.

When a value is cast to a number, if it is a string containing characters other than digits (or for another reason it cannot be converted to a number) then the JavaScript value NaN (for Not a Number) will be returned by Number(), instead of a number. Since NaN values cannot have arithmetic operations performed on them any attempt to do so will see the value remain as NaN, so the following results in MyVar containing the value NaN, and not the value 23 as you might expect:

```
MyVar = Number("A string") + 23
```

The String() function is the most flexible in that it can safely turn any value into a string, even including JavaScript values such as NaN, null, undefined, true and false.

Summary

We've actually covered quite a lot of ground in this lecture, which has explained some of the simpler JavaScript syntax and data handling capabilities. In the following lecture we'll start to see how these come together with operators to enable you to start creating simple JavaScript expressions.

JavaScript Operators

By following this lecture you will:

- ✓ *Be able to use operators effectively.*
- ✓ *Know how to combine assignments with operators.*
- ✓ *Understand the reason for operator precedence.*

IN THE PREVIOUS lecture you have already seen a few examples of operators in action, such as the + sign used either for addition, or for concatenating strings together, the – sign used for subtraction, and the = operator used for assigning values.

But JavaScript supports many more operators than that, such as *, / and more, and also includes functions you can draw on for more advanced expression evaluation, such as `Math.sin()`, `Math.sqrt()`, and many others. In this lecture I'll explain all of these, how they work and how to use them.

This is an important lecture since it covers much of the foundation of how JavaScript works so, even if you have programmed before using another language, I recommend you read this thoroughly, because there are a number of things JavaScript handles in a unique manner.

Arithmetic Operators

The arithmetic operators in JavaScript are the ones that allow you to create numeric expressions and there are more than simply addition, subtraction, multiplication and division, as shown in Table 4-1.

Operator	Description	Example	Result
+	Addition	3 + 11	14
-	Subtraction	9 - 4	5
*	Multiplication	3 * 4	12
/	Division	21 / 7	3
%	Modulus (*remainder after division*)	21 % 8	5
++	Increment	a = 5; ++a	(a *equals*) 6
--	Decrement	a = 5; --a	(a *equals*) 4

Table 1: The arithmetic operators.

You can try these operators out for yourself by loading the file *math_operators.htm* from the companion archive into a browser, which should look like Figure 4-1. Try changing the various values and operators applied, and check the results you get.

The first four of these operators should be very clear to you so I'll only explain the last three, starting with the modulus operator, %. What this operator returns is simply the remainder after calculating a division. For example, the modulus of 12 and 4, calculated using the expression 12 % 4, is 0, because 4 goes into 12 an exact number of times, and therefore there is no remainder.

On the other hand, the modulus of 24 and 5 (calculated as 24 % 5) is 4, because 5 goes into 24 four times (5 × 4 is 20), leaving a remainder of 4, the modulus of the expression.

Now let's look at the increment and decrement operators. These come in tremendously handy because without them you would have to write expressions like this:

```
a = a + 1
```

This is cumbersome when you only want to increment (or decrement) a value by 1, and so the creators of JavaScript allow you to use the following syntax instead:

```
++a
```

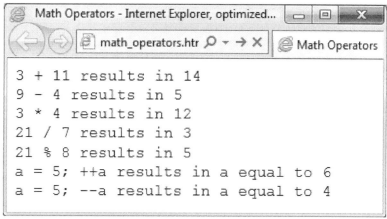

Figure 1: The arithmetic operators in use.

I'm sure you will agree this is much shorter and sweeter. It also comes with fringe benefits too, because the increment and decrement operators can be used within flow control commands such as `if()` statements (which I explain in full detail in Lecture 8, but will give you a taster here).

Consider the following code, which assumes that Time contains a 24-hour time value between 0 and 23, and which is set up to trigger once an hour, on the hour (using code not shown here, but which is assumed to be in place):

```
Time = Time + 1
document.write('The time is ' + Time)
if (Time < 12) document.write('AM')
else            document.write('PM')
```

This code first increments the value in `Time` by 1, because this code has been called on the hour, so it's now one hour since the last time it was called, and so `Time` must be updated. Then on the next line it displays the time in the browser (using a call to the `document.write()` function) prefaced by the string `'The time is '`.

After that an `if()` statement is reached which tests the variable `Time` to see whether it currently has a value of less than 12. If so then it must still be the morning and so the string `'AM'` is output. Otherwise it's the afternoon and so `'PM'` is displayed – fairly straight-forward stuff.

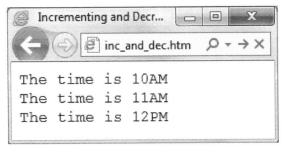

Figure 2: Using the increment operator.

Note: *This is a simple version of the* if() *statement in that it has only a single statement after the* if, *and there is also only a single one after* else. *Therefore no curly braces are used to enclose the action statements. Please see Lecture 8 for more details on using* if() and else *with multi-statement actions.*

However programmers always like to write the tightest and cleanest code possible, and so the following code is considered better programming practice, as it removes an entire line of code, like this (with the incremented variable and operator highlighted):

```
document.write('The time is ' + ++Time)

if (Time < 12) document.write('AM')
else           document.write('PM')
```

Pre-Incrementing

What has occurred in the previous example is an instance of *pre-incrementing* the variable Time. In other words, before the value in Time is used it is incremented. Only after this incrementing is the current value in Time used for displaying in the document.write() statement.

In Figure 4-2 these three lines of code have been called three times, with an original starting value for Time of 9 (using the file *inc_and_dec.htm* from the companion archive).

Post-Incrementing

You may also place the ++ increment operator after a variable name, and then it is known as *post-incrementing*. What happens when you do this is that the value in the variable being incremented is looked up before the increment, and that value is used by the code accessing it. Only after this value has been looked up is the variable incremented.

The following code illustrates this type of incrementing by displaying both the before and after values in the variable a (with instances of the variable and increment operator highlighted):

```
document.write('a was ' + a++ + ' and is now ' + a)
```

Working through this statement from left to right, first the string 'a was ' is output, then a++ is displayed. This results in the current value of a being displayed, and only then is a incremented. After this the string ' and is now ' is output, followed by the new value in a, which now contains the incremented value from the earlier increment operation. So, if a had an initial value of 10, then the following is displayed:

```
a is 10 and is now 11
```

Pre- and Post-Decrementing

You can use the decrement operator in exactly the same way as the increment operator, and it can either be placed before a variable for pre-incrementing, or after for post-decrementing. Following are two examples that both display the same but achieve the result using pre-decrementing for the first, and post-decrementing for the second (with instances of the variable and decrement operator highlighted):

```
document.write('b is ' + b + ' and is now ' + --b)
document.write('b is ' + b-- + ' and is now ' + b)
```

Here, if b had an initial value of 10, then the following is displayed:

```
b is 10 and is now 9
b is 9 and is now 8
```

Note: If it's still not entirely clear which type of increment or decrement operator to use out of pre- and post- methods, don't worry, just use the pre- methods (with the operator before the variable) for now, because it will become obvious to you when the time comes that you actually have a need to use the post- method (with the operator after the variable).

Arithmetic Functions

To accompany the arithmetic operators, JavaScript comes with a Math library of functions you can call on:

- `Math.abs(a)` Returns a as a positive number
- `Math.acos(a)` Returns the arc cosine of a.
- `Math.asin(a)` Returns the arc sine of a.
- `Math.atan(a)` Returns the arc tangent of a.
- `Math.atan2(a,b)` Returns the arc tangent of a / b.
- `Math.ceil(a)` Rounds up to return the integer closest to a.
- `Math.cos(a)` Returns the cosine of a.
- `Math.exp(a)` Returns the exponent of a (`Math.E` to the power a).
- `Math.floor(a)` Rounds down to return the integer closest to a.
- `Math.log(a)` Returns the log of a base e.
- `Math.max(a,b)` Returns the maximum of a and b.
- `Math.min(a,b)` Returns the minimum of a and b.
- `Math.pow(a,b)` Returns a to the power b.
- `Math.random()` Returns a random number between 0 and 0.999 (*recurring*).
- `Math.round(a)` Rounds up or down to return the integer closest to a.
- `Math.sin(a)` Returns the sine of a.
- `Math.sqrt(a)` Returns the square root of a.
- `Math.tan(a)` Returns the tangent of a.

You should be familiar with most of these, for example, to return the square root of 64 you would use the following:

```
Math.sqrt(64) // Returns 8
```

But there are a couple that need a little more explaining, such as `Math.abs()`. What this does is take any value (negative, zero or positive), and if it is negative turns in into a positive value, like this:

```
Math.abs(27)  // Returns 27
Math.abs(0)   // Returns 0
Math.abs(-5)  // Returns 5
```

The other function needing extra explanation is `Math.random()`. This returns a floating point value with a statistically random value (although not truly random) between 0 and 1. So, for example, if you have to emulate a 12-sided dice you must multiply the result of the function call and turn it into an integer, like this:

```
Math.floor(Math.random() * 12) // Returns 0 - 11
```

This expression returns a value between 0 and 11.999 recurring, which is first turned into an integer, by dropping the floating point part of the number using the `Math.float()` function. The result is a value between 0 and 11.

Note: If, for example, you need your random number to be a value between 1 and 12 (rather than 0 through 11) simply add 1 to this result.

Assignment Operators

Like many other languages JavaScript likes to help you out by offering more efficient ways to achieve results. One of these ways is by letting you combine assignment and arithmetic operators together into six different types of assignment operator.

This typically saves lines of code and makes your program code much easier to write, and for others to understand.

Table 4-2 lists the assignment operators available, provides examples of them in use and shows the result of doing so when the variable a already contains the value 21.

You can see the result of using the expressions in this table in Figure 4-3, created with the example file *assignment_operators.htm* from the accompanying archive.

Operator	Description	Example	Result in a
=	Simple Assignment	a = 42	42
+=	With Addition	a += 5	26
-=	With Subtraction	a -= 2	19
*=	With Multiplication	a *= 3	63
/=	With Division	a /= 10	2.1
%=	With Modulus	a %= 4	1

Table 2: The assignment operators.

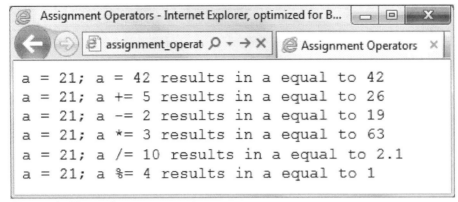

Figure 3: Using the various assignment operators.

So, for example, instead of using a = a + 5, you can use the more compact a += 5. And you can use assignment operators in conjunction with other expressions and variables, as with the following example, which results in a having a value of 15 (10 + (25 / 5)):

```
a   = 10
b   = 25
a += (b / 5)
```

Operator	Description	Example	Result
==	Equal to	1 == 1	true
===	Equal in value & type	1 === '1'	false
!=	Not equal to	1 != 2	true
!==	Not equal in value & type	1 !== '1'	true
>	Greater than	1 > 2	false
<	Less than	1 < 2	true
>=	Greater than or equal to	1 >= 1	true
<=	Less than or equal to	2 <= 1	false

Table 3: The comparison operators.

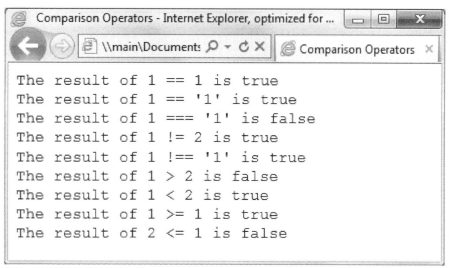

Figure 4: A selection of comparison operators in use.

Comparison Operators

One of the most important process that happens in a program is comparison. For example, possible the most frequent type of construct used goes along the lines of *if this then do that*. The job of comparison operators is to figure out the *this* part, and there are eight of them, as listed in Table 4-3.

Figure 4-4 shows several different comparison operators used on different values and the results obtained. It was created using the file *comparison_operators.htm*, available in the companion archive.

If you haven't programmed before, some of these operators may seem a little confusing, especially seeing as we are taught as children that = is the equal to operator. However, in programming languages such as JavaScript the = is used as an assignment operator, and therefore code would become harder to read (and the writers of programming languages would have a much harder time figuring out its meaning) if the = symbol were also used to make comparisons. Therefore the == operator is used for comparisons instead, like this:

```
if (a == 12) // Do something
```

In JavaScript, however, the types of variables are loosely defined and it's quite normal, for example, to ask whether 1 is the same as '1', because the string '1' can be used either as a string or as a number depending on the context. Therefore the following expression will return the value true:

```
if (1 == '1') // Results in the value true
```

Note: JavaScript uses the internal values of true and false to represent the result of making comparisons such as the preceding, and you can use the keywords true and false in your programming to check for these values.

Progressing through the list of comparison operators, when you wish to determine whether two values are the same value and *also* of the same type, you can use the === operator, like this:

```
if (1 === '1') // Results in the value false
```

Similarly you can test whether values are *not* equal (but not comparing the type) using the != operator, like this:

```
if (1 != 2)    // Results in the value true
if (1 != '1') // Results in the value false
```

And if you wish to check whether two values are not equal in *both* value and type you use the !== operator, like this:

```
if (1 !== '1') // Results in the value true
```

The remaining comparison operators test whether one value is greater than, less then, greater than or equal to, or less than or equal to another, like this:

```
if (1 > 2)  // Results in the value false
if (1 < 2)  // Results in the value true
if (1 >= 1) // Results in the value true
if (2 <= 1) // Results in the value false
```

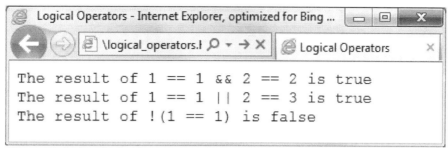

The result of 1 == 1 && 2 == 2 is true
The result of 1 == 1 || 2 == 3 is true
The result of !(1 == 1) is false

Figure 5: Using logical operators.

Logical Operators

JavaScript supports three logical operators with which you can extend your *if this* parts of code even further, as listed in Table 4-4:

Figure 4-5, created using the file *logical_operators.htm* from the companion archive, shows these operators being used in expressions.

The `&&` operator (known as the and operator) allows you to test for multiple conditions being `true`, saving you from having to write multiple lines of code by combining them into a single expression, like this:

```
if (a == 4 && b == 7) // Do this
```

In this example the statement following the `if()` (just a comment in this instance) will be executed only if `a` has a value of 4 and also `b` has a value of 7. Or you can test whether at least one value is `true` using the `||` operator (known as the or operator), like this:

```
if (a == 4 || b == 7) // Do this
```

Operator	Description	Example	Result
&&	And	1 == 1 && 2 == 2	true
||	Or	1 == 1 || 2 == 3	true
!	Not	!(1 == 1)	false

Table 4: The logical operators.

Here if either a has the value 4 or b has the value 7 then the statement after the `if()` will be executed, so only one of the expressions needs to evaluate to `true`. Finally you can negate any expression using the `!` symbol (known as the not operator) by placing it in front of the expression (generally placing the expression within brackets too, so that the `!` doesn't apply only to a part of the expression), like this:

```
if (!(game == over)) // Carry on playing
```

In this example, if the variable game contains the same value as the variable over the result of the expression is `true`. Then the `!` operator negates this to turn that value into `false`. Therefore the statement after the `if()` will not be executed.

On the other hand, if game is not equal to over then the expression evaluates to `false`, which is negated to true, and so the code after the `if()` is executed. Therefore the expression equates to the semi-English sentence "If not game over then do this".

Note: When an expression can only return either a `true` or `false` value it is known as a Boolean expression. When combined with and, or and not (`&&` and `||` and `!`) such expressions are said to use Boolean logic.

The Ternary Operator

Ever on the lookout for ways to make program code simpler and more compact, program language developers also came up with a thing called the ternary operator, which allows you to combine "If this then do that thing otherwise do another thing" type logic into a single expression, like this:

```
document.write(game == over ? 'Game over' : 'Keep playing')
```

The way the ternary operator works is that you provide an expression that can return either `true` or `false` (a Boolean expression). Following this you put a `?` character, after which you place the two options, separated with a `:` character, as follows:

```
expression ? do this : do that
```

For example, another ternary expression might go like the following, which sets the string variable AmPm to either `'AM'` or `'PM'`, according to the numeric value in the variable Time:

```
AmPm = Time < 12 ? 'AM' : 'PM'
```

Bitwise Operators

There is a type of operator supported by JavaScript that as a beginner to programming you are most unlikely to use, due to it being quite advanced, and that's the bitwise operator. This type of operator acts on the individual 0 and 1 bits that make up binary numbers, and can be quite tricky to use.

The bitwise operators are &, |, ^, ~, <<, >> and >>>. In order they support bitwise and, or, exclusive or, not, left-shift, sign-propagating right-shift and zero-fill right-shift on binary numbers.

The bitwise operators can be combined with the = assignment operator to make a whole new collection of bitwise assignment operators.

However, this is a crash course on JavaScript and not an advanced tutorial so I shan't go into how you use them, because you already have enough new stuff to learn as it is. But for the curious who would like to know more about them, you can check out the following web pages which cover them in some detail:

tinyurl.com/bitwiseops
tinyurl.com/bitwiseops2

Operator Precedence

In JavaScript some operators are given a higher precedence than others. For example, multiplication has a higher precedence than addition, so in the following expression the multiplication will occur *before* the addition, even though the addition appears first:

```
3 + 4 * 5
```

The result of this expression is 23 (4 * 5 is 20, 3 + 20 is 23). But if there were no operator precedence (with the expression executed simply from left to right) it would evaluate to 35 (3 + 4 is 7, 7 * 5 is 35).

By providing precedence to operators it obviates the need for parentheses, since the only way to make the preceding expression come out to 23 without operator precedence would be to insert parentheses as follows:

```
3 + (4 * 5)
```

Precedence	Operators	Precedence	Operators
1	`. [] new`	10	`&`
2	`()`	11	`^`
3	`++ --`	12	`|`
4	`! ~ unary+ unary-` `typeof void delete`	13	`&&`
5	`* / %`	14	`||`
6	`+ -`	15	`?:`

7	`<< >> >>>`	16	`= += -= *= /= %=`
			`<<= >>= >>>= &= ^=`
			`!=`

8	`< <= > >= in` `instanceof`	17	`,`
9	`== != === !==`		

Table 5: Operator precedence.

With this concept in mind, the creators of JavaScript have divided all the operators up into varying levels of precedence according to how 'important' they are (in that multiplication is considered more 'important' than addition due to its greater ability to create larger numbers). For the same reason division is given greater precedence than subtraction, and so on.

Therefore, unless you intend to use parentheses in all your expressions to ensure the correct precedence (which would make your code much harder to write, and for others to understand, due to multiple levels of parentheses), you need to know these precedencies, which are listed in Table 4-5:

There are quite a few operators in this table that you haven't seen yet. Some of which (such as the bitwise operators) I will not be covering, and others that will be explained later in the course (such as `in`, `typeof` and so on).

All you need to learn from this table, though, is which operators have higher precedence than others, where 1 is the highest and 17 is the lowest precedence, and where an operator has lower precedence but you need to elevate it, all you need to do is apply parentheses in the right places for the operators within them to have raised precedence:

Note: The `unary+` *and* `unary-` *entries in Table 4-5 represent the use of placing either a + before an expression to force it into being used as a number, or placing a – sign in front of an expression to negate it (change a negative value to positive or vice versa). The comma operator (at a precedence of 17) is used as an expression or argument separator, so it naturally has the lowest precedence.*

Operator Associativity

JavaScript operators also have an attribute known as associativity, which is the direction in which they should be evaluated. For example, the assignment operators all have right-to-left associativity because you are assigning the value on the right to the variable on the left, like this:

```
MyVar = 0
```

Because of this right-to-left associativity you can string assignments together, setting more than one variable at a time to a given value, like this:

```
MyVar = ThatVar = OtherVar = 0
```

This works because associativity of assignments starts at the right and continues in a leftward direction. In this instance `OtherVar` is first assigned the value 0. Then `ThatVar` is assigned the value in `OtherVar`, and finally `MyVar` is assigned the value in `ThatVar`.

On the other hand, some operators have left-to-right associativity, such as the `||` (or) operator for example. You see, because of left-to-right associativity the process of executing JavaScript can be speeded up, as demonstrated in the following example:

```
if (ThisVar == 1 || ThatVar == 1) // Do this
```

When JavaScript encounters the `||` operator it knows to check the left-hand side first. So, if `ThisVar` has a value of 1 there is no need to look up the value of `ThatVar`, because as long as one or the other expression either side of the `||` operator evaluates to `true`, the `||` expression evaluates to `true`, and if the left half has evaluated to

Associativity	Operators
right-to-left	! ~ unary+ unary- typeof void delete ?: = += -= *= /= %= <<= >>= >>>= &= ^= |=
left-to-right	. [] * / % + - << >> >>> < <= > >= in instanceof == != === !== & ^ | && || ,

Table 6: Operator associativity.

`true`, so has the whole `||` expression. In cases such as this, the JavaScript interpreter will eagerly skip the second half of the expression, knowing it is running in an optimised fashion.

Knowing whether operators have right-to-left or left-to-right associativity can really help your programming. For example, if you are using a left-to-right associative operator such as `||` you can line up all your expressions left to right from the most to the least important.

Therefore it's worth taking a moment to familiarise yourself with the contents of Table 4-6, so that you will know which operators have what associativity.

The `with` Keyword

Using JavaScript's `with` keyword you can simplify some types of JavaScript statements by reducing many references to an object to a single reference. For example, in the following code the `document.write()` function never references the variable `string` by name:

```
string = "The quick brown fox jumps over the lazy dog"

with (string)
{
   document.write("The string's length is " + length)
   document.write("<br />Upper case: " + toUpperCase())
}
```

Even though `string` is never directly referenced by `document.write()`, this code still manages to output the following:

> The string's length is 43 characters
> Upper case: THE QUICK BROWN FOX JUMPS OVER THE LAZY DOG

The way this works is that the JavaScript interpreter recognizes that the `length` property and the `toUpperCase()` method have to be applied to some object, but because they stand alone the interpreter assumes they must apply to the `string` object specified in the `with` statement.

Note: The very fact that assumptions about which object to apply the `with` to have to be made by the interpreter, can make its use ambiguous in some applications. Therefore I would generally recommend that you try to avoid working with this statement until you feel confident that you can use it without ambiguity.

Summary

This lecture has brought you up to scratch with all you need to know about using operators, so now you're ready to start looking at some of JavaScript's more complex and interesting objects in the following lecture on arrays.

JavaScript Arrays

By following this lecture you will:

- ✓ *Be able to use numeric and string arrays for storing values.*
- ✓ *Understand how to add and retrieve array data.*
- ✓ *Know how to handle associative arrays.*

JAVASCRIPT IS CAPABLE of managing data in a more powerful manner than simply via variables. One example of this is JavaScript arrays, which you can think of as collections of variables grouped together. For example, a good metaphor for an array might be a filing cabinet with each drawer representing a different variable, as shown in Figure 5-1.

As with the small pot metaphor in Lecture 3, with the filing cabinet to assign a value you should imagine writing it down on pieces of paper, placing it in the relevant drawer and closing it. To read back a value you open the drawer, take out the paper, read its value, return the paper and close the drawer. The only difference between the cabinet and the pots is that the drawers of the filing cabinet (representing an array) are all in sequential order, whereas a collection of pots (representing variables) are stored in no particular order.

Although JavaScript arrays can be any size (up to the available memory in your computer), for the sake of simplicity I have only shown ten elements in the figure. You can access each of the elements in an array numerically, starting with element 0 (the top drawer of the cabinet). This index number is important, because you might think that logically the number 1 would be the best starting point, but that isn't how JavaScript arrays are accessed – you should always remember that the first element is the zeroth.

Figure 1: A filing cabinet representing a 10-element array.

Array Names

The rules for naming arrays are exactly the same as those for naming variables. Array names must begin with either an upper or lower case letter (a-z or A-Z), or the $ or _ symbols. No other character may begin an array name.

Array names may not contain any mathematical operators (such as + or *), punctuation (such as ! or &), or spaces, but after the first character they may include the digits 0-9 or any of the characters that can begin an array or variable name.

All JavaScript keywords (such as window, open, string, and so on) are reserved and may not be used as array names.

Creating an Array

To create an array you can declare it in advance to initialize it, like this:

```
MyArray = new Array()
```

This has the effect of creating a new object of the type `Array()` and then calling it `MyArray`. This array object contains no data but is ready for data to be assigned to its elements.

Creating an Array of Specific Length

To create an array of a specific length, you provide a single argument to the `Array()` function call, like this:

```
MyArray = new Array(5)
```

This has the effect of creating a new object of the type `Array()` and then calling it `MyArray`. This array object contains no data but has five elements ready to be populated with values.

Assigning Values to an Array Element

You can populate arrays with data (in a similar manner to assigning values to variables) like this:

```
MyArray[0] = 23 MyArray[1] = 67.35
```

Here the integer 23 is assigned to element 0 (the top drawer of the cabinet), while the floating point number 67.35 is assigned to the index at element 1 (the second drawer down – because they begin at 0). In fact you can assign any legal value to an array element, including strings, objects, and even other arrays (which I'll come to in Lecture 5), like this:

```
MyArray[3] = "Hello world"
MyArray[4] = new Date()
```

Note: I explain the use of objects in Lecture 11, but for now all you need know is that MyArray[4] now contains a Date object holding the current date and time. You are not restricted to assigning values in order, so you can go right in and assign values to any elements, like this:

```
MyArray[9] = "Good morning"
MyArray[7] = 3.1415927
```

Using Indexes

The element number used for storing a particular value is known as the array *index*, and you can use integer (as shown so far) or variable values as indexes. For example, the following first creates a variable and assigns it a numeric value, which is then used to assign another value to the array:

```
MyIndex          = 123
MyArray[MyIndex] = "Good evening"
```

This has the effect of assigning the string value "Good evening" to the element with an index of 123 in `MyArray[]`.

Retrieving Values

Once an array has been created and it has been populated with data, to retrieve a value from an array you simply refer to it, like this:

```
document.write(MyArray[0])
```

This will fetch the value stored in the zeroth element of `MyArray[]` (or the top drawer of the filing cabinet metaphor) and then pass it to the `document.write()` function to display it in the browser. You can, likewise, return a value using a variable, like this:

```
MyIndex = 713
document.write(MyArray[MyIndex])
```

Whatever value is stored in element 713 of the array will then be displayed in the browser.

Note: The preceding two examples (and many following ones) assume you have already created an array. If you have not previously created an array but try to read from one, an error will be generated and your code will fail.

There are other ways you can use array values, such as assigning them to other variables or other array elements, or using them in expressions. For example, the following code assigns the value 23 to an array element, which is then looked up and used in an expression, in which 50 is added to it and the result (73) is displayed in the browser:

```
MyArray[7] = 23
document write(MyArray[7] + 50)
```

Figure 2: Displaying a value in an alert window.

Or, you may wish to display a value in an alert window using code such as the following, which results in your browser looking like Figure 5-2 (although the style of the window varies by browser):

```
MyArray[7] = 23
alert(MyArray[7] + 50)
```

Using Array Elements as Indexes

You can even go a step further and use the value stored in an array element as an index into another (or the same) array, like this:

```
OtherArray[0]             = 77
MyArray[OtherArray[0]] = "I love the movie Inception"
```

Here the zeroth element of `OtherArray[]` is assigned the integer value of 77. Once assigned, this element is used as the index into `MyArray[]` (rather like the movie *Inception*, with arrays within arrays). However, this is quite complex programming and you are unlikely to use these types of indexes as a beginner to JavaScript.

Note: The fact that you can use any valid integer value (including values in variables, array elements and those returned by functions) means that you can use mathematical equations to iterate through arrays. For example, as you will discover in Lecture 8, it is easy to create code that runs in a loop to process each element of an array in turn.

Other Ways of Creating Arrays

You have already seen the following type of declaration for creating a JavaScript array:

```
MyArray = new Array()
```

But there are also a couple of other methods you can use, which also have the effect of simplifying your code, by allowing you to populate the array with some data at the same time. The first method is as follows:

```
MyArray = new Array(123, "Hello there", 3.21)
```

Here the array `MyArray[]` is created and its first three elements immediately populated with three different values: an integer, a string and a floating point number. This is equivalent to the following (much longer) code:

```
MyArray       = new Array()
MyArray[0] = 123
MyArray[1] = "Hello there"
MyArray[2] = 3.21
```

You can also go a step further and simplify things right down to their bare bones, by using code that implies the creating of an array, without employing the `new` keyword or the `Array()` function, like this:

```
MyArray = [123, "Hello there", 3.21]
```

Note: Once you have created an array, if you need to apply any more values to elements within it, you must use the standard form of assigning values. If you re-use the short form of combined array creation and value assignment, it will simply reset the array to the values in the assignment.

Using Associative Arrays

Using numeric indexes is all well and good when you only have a few elements in an array to cope with. But once an array starts to hold meaningful amounts of data, using numbers to access its elements can be highly confusing. Thankfully JavaScript provides a great solution to this by supporting the use of names to associate with array elements, in much the same way that variables have names.

Let's use JavaScript's associative arrays to store the ages of the players in a mixed, under eleven, five-a-side soccer team. Here the array is initialized and then the age of each player is assigned to an element in the array using the player's names:

```
SoccerTeam = new Array()
SoccerTeam['Andy']  = 10
SoccerTeam['Brian'] = 8
SoccerTeam['Cathy'] = 9
SoccerTeam['David'] = 10
SoccerTeam['Ellen'] = 9
```

Having been assigned, these values they can now easily be looked up by name, like this, which displays Cathy's age in the browser:

```
document.write(SoccerTeam['Cathy'])
```

Keys, Values, and Hash Tables

When you use associative arrays you are actually creating a collection of *key* and *value* pairs. The name you assign to an array element is known as the key, while the value you provide to the element is the value.

In other languages (such as PHP) this type of data structure is known as a *hash table*. When an object (such as a string) is used as a key for a value this is called a hash value, and the data structure is a hash table. Later on, in Lecture 11, you will learn how all variables in JavaScript are, in fact, objects and that you can access them in a variety of ways, as well as those I have so far shown you (variables, arrays and associative arrays).

Other Ways of Creating an Associative Array

If you wish, you can use a short from of creating and populating an associative array, like this:

```
SoccerTeam = new Array(
{
  'Andy'  : 10,
  'Brian' : 8,
  'Cathy' : 9,
  'David' : 10,
  'Ellen' : 9
})
```

Note: The syntax here is different from populating a standard array, in that you must enclose the element value assignments in curly braces. If you use the square braces instead the statement will fail. Also, rather than using = you use the : operator to assign values.

In fact, you can shorten the syntax even further by having your code imply the new keyword and `Array()` function, like this:

```
SoccerTeam =
{
   'Andy'  : 10,
   'Brian' : 8,
   'Cathy' : 9,
   'David' : 10,
   'Ellen' : 9
}
```

I'm sure you'll agree this is much simpler and easier to use, once you know that this type of code structure causes the creation of an array. But you may prefer to stick with the longer form until you are completely happy with using arrays. Also, I have chosen to be liberal with newlines here for reasons of clarity, but if you wish you can run all these five sub-statements into a single line.

As with standard variables and arrays, you are not restricted to only storing numbers in associative arrays, because you can assign any valid value, including integers, floating point numbers, strings, and even other arrays and objects. The following illustrates a couple of these:

```
MyInfo =
{
   'Name'        : 'Bill Gates',
   'Age'         : 56,
   'Occupation'  : 'Philanthropist',
   'Children'    : 3,
   'Worth'       : 59000000000
}
```

In the preceding example both strings and numbers have been assigned to the array elements. You can read back any value simply by referring to it, like this, which displays the value in `'Occupation'` (namely `'Philanthropist'`) in the browser:

```
document.write(MyInfo['Occupation'])
```

Note: In Lecture 11 you will learn how JavaScript arrays are actually examples of objects (as are all JavaScript variables), and how they can be used in Object Oriented Programming (OOP).

Summary

By now you'll have a pretty good understanding of JavaScript arrays and will be beginning to see how they can make excellent structures for handling your data. In the following lecture I'll show you how there's actually a lot more to arrays than you've so far seen, and we'll begin to make some reasonably complex data objects.

MULTIDIMENSIONAL ARRAYS

By following this lecture you will:

- ✓ *Be able to use more than one level of nested arrays.*
- ✓ *Know how to create associative multidimensional arrays.*
- ✓ *Be familiar with populating large arrays with data.*

LET ME START by totally contradicting the title of this lecture and stating that there's actually no such thing as multidimensional arrays in JavaScript. But before you start scratching your head and wondering whether I've drunk too many cups of tea, let me say that you can *simulate* multidimensional arrays in JavaScript by assigning new arrays as the values for elements of an existing array.

But what exactly do I mean by *multidimensional* in the first place? Well, in the same way that a string of characters is a collection of individual letters, numbers and other characters, that you can imagine being like a string of pearls – with each pearl occupying its right location, and the correct pearls on either side, all in the right order, an array, therefore, is like a collection of variables all stored in their right locations.

In the previous chapter I used the metaphor of a filing cabinet for an array of ten elements. If you imagine for a moment that each drawer in this filing cabinet is like *Doctor Who*'s Tardis (his time and space machine) in that it is much bigger on the inside than it is on the

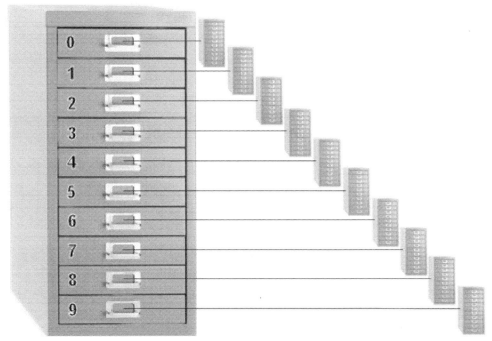

Figure 1: Representing a two-dimensional array with filing cabinets.

outside, then you should be able to also imagine being able to place another ten-drawer filing cabinet in each of the drawers of the original one! Figure 6-1 should help make this clearer.

Remember that these particular filing cabinets are not bound by the normal rules of space and time, so that the small cabinets can contain just as much as the large one.

In fact the cabinets are capable of holding an infinite amount of data, limited only by the restraints of your browser, operating system and available memory.

I have simply drawn the secondary filing cabinets much smaller so that they fit into the figure.

Creating a Two-Dimensional Array

Let's see how we can use the ability of an array element being able to store another entire array to our advantage by considering a ten times multiplication table, just like those often found on the walls of school children (see Figure 6-2).

	1	2	3	4	5	6	7	8	9	10
1	1	2	3	4	5	6	7	8	9	10
2	2	4	6	8	10	12	14	16	18	20
3	3	6	9	12	15	18	21	24	27	30
4	4	8	12	16	20	24	28	32	36	40
5	5	10	15	20	25	30	35	40	45	50
6	6	12	18	24	30	36	42	48	54	60
7	7	14	21	28	35	42	49	56	63	70
8	8	16	24	32	40	48	56	64	72	80
9	9	18	27	36	45	54	63	72	81	90
10	10	20	40	40	50	60	70	80	90	100

Figure 2: A ten times multiplication table.

Each of the columns (or each of the rows) can be considered a one-dimensional array. For example, the first row could be created using the following code:

```
MyTable0      = new Array()
MyTable0[0]  = 1
MyTable1[1]  = 2
MyTable2[2]  = 3
MyTable3[3]  = 4
MyTable4[4]  = 5
MyTable5[5]  = 6
MyTable6[6]  = 7
MyTable7[7]  = 8
MyTable8[8]  = 9
MyTable9[9]  = 10
```

Or, more succinctly:

```
MyTable0 = [1, 2, 3, 4, 5, 6, 7, 8, 9, 10]
```

Similarly, the second row could be created like this:

```
MyTable1 = [2, 4, 6, 8, 10, 12, 14, 16, 18, 20]
```

And so you can go on for rows three through ten, so that you end up with the following set of statements:

```
MyTable0 = [ 1,  2,  3,  4,  5,  6,  7,  8,  9, 10]
MyTable1 = [ 2,  4,  6,  8, 10, 12, 14, 16, 18, 20]
MyTable2 = [ 3,  6,  9, 12, 15, 18, 21, 24, 27, 20]
MyTable3 = [ 4,  8, 12, 16, 20, 24, 28, 32, 36, 20]
MyTable4 = [ 5, 10, 15, 20, 25, 30, 35, 40, 45, 20]
MyTable5 = [ 6, 12, 18, 24, 30, 36, 42, 48, 54, 20]
MyTable6 = [ 7, 14, 21, 28, 35, 42, 49, 56, 63, 20]
MyTable7 = [ 8, 16, 24, 32, 40, 48, 56, 64, 72, 20]
MyTable8 = [ 9, 18, 27, 36, 45, 54, 63, 72, 81, 20]
MyTable9 = [10, 20, 30, 40, 50, 60, 70, 80, 90,100]
```

At this point we now have 10 arrays – one for each row in the times table. With these now created, it is now possible to build a two-dimensional table by creating just one more, master, table, like this:

```
MasterTable     = new Array()
MasterTable[0] = MyTable0
MasterTable[1] = MyTable1
MasterTable[2] = MyTable2
MasterTable[3] = MyTable3
MasterTable[4] = MyTable4
MasterTable[5] = MyTable5
MasterTable[6] = MyTable6
MasterTable[7] = MyTable7
MasterTable[8] = MyTable8
MasterTable[9] = MyTable9
```

Or by using the shorter form of:

```
MasterTable =
[
  MyTable0,
  MyTable1,
  MyTable2,
  MyTable3,
  MyTable4,
  MyTable5,
  MyTable6,
  MyTable7,
  MyTable8,
  MyTable9
]
```

Note: I have chosen to split this up into multiple lines for clarity, but you can equally include all the preceding in a single statement on one line.

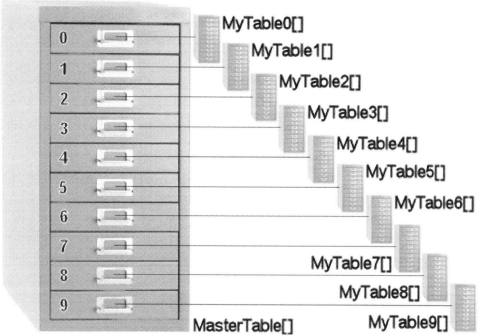

Figure 3: The relationship between the cabinets and arrays.

Accessing a Two-Dimensional Array

Let's now look at how this relates to the filing cabinets in Figure 6-1 in terms of code. To recap, there's a main array called `MasterTable[]`, and its ten elements each contain another array named `MyTable0[]` through `MyTable9[]`.

As you will recall from the previous chapter, accessing an array is as simple as the following, which displays the value in the array held at a numeric index of 23 (which will be element 24 since arrays start from 0) in an alert window:

```
alert(SomeArray[23])
```

But what should you do when the value stored in an array element is another array? The answer is simple and elegant – you simply add another pair of square brackets following the first pair, and place an index value into that new array between them, like this:

```
alert(MasterTable[0][0])
```

This statement opens an alert window and displays in it the contents of the first element of the array that is stored in the first element of `MasterTable[]`. Notice that there is no need to reference the sub-array (sub-array being the term I use for referring to arrays within arrays) by name.

Likewise, if you wish to display the value held in the seventh row of the array stored in the third element of MasterTable[] you would use code such as this (remembering that table indexes start at 0 not 1, so the seventh and third elements will be 6 and 2 respectively):

```
alert(MasterTable[2][6])
```

In terms of the times table in Figure 56-2 this is equivalent to first moving to the seventh column along, and then down to the third row, at which point you can see that the value shown is 21, as you will quickly see if you look at the source of *timestable.htm* (available in the companion archive):

```
<!DOCTYPE html>
<html>
  <head>
    <title>Two-Dimensional Array Example</title>
  </head>
  <body>
    <script>
      MyTable0 = [ 1,  2,  3,  4,  5,  6,  7,  8,  9, 10]
      MyTable1 = [ 2,  4,  6,  8, 10, 12, 14, 16, 18, 20]
      MyTable2 = [ 3,  6,  9, 12, 15, 18, 21, 24, 27, 20]
      MyTable3 = [ 4,  8, 12, 16, 20, 24, 28, 32, 36, 20]
      MyTable4 = [ 5, 10, 15, 20, 25, 30, 35, 40, 45, 20]
      MyTable5 = [ 6, 12, 18, 24, 30, 36, 42, 48, 54, 20]
      MyTable6 = [ 7, 14, 21, 28, 35, 42, 49, 56, 63, 20]
      MyTable7 = [ 8, 16, 24, 32, 40, 48, 56, 64, 72, 20]
      MyTable8 = [ 9, 18, 27, 36, 45, 54, 63, 72, 81, 20]
      MyTable9 = [10, 20, 30, 40, 50, 60, 70, 80, 90,100]

      MasterTable = [MyTable0, MyTable1, MyTable2,
                     MyTable3, MyTable4, MyTable5,
                     MyTable6, MyTable7, MyTable8,
                     MyTable9]
      alert('The value at location 2,6 is ' +
        MasterTable[2][6])
    </script>
  </body>
</html>
```

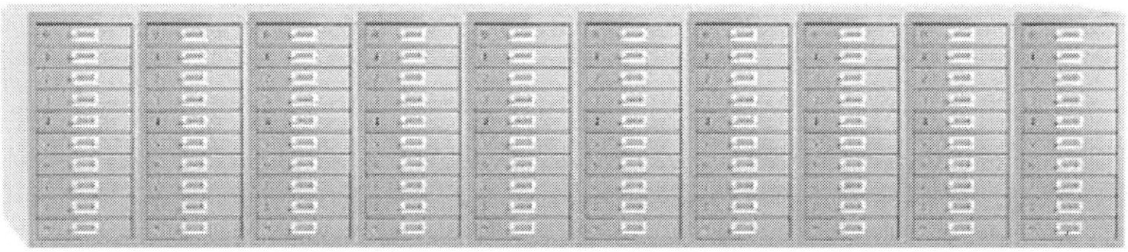

Figure 4: The small filing cabinets are now lined up alongside each other.

Note: *This code is equivalent to the filing cabinets in Figure 6-1, in that the* `MasterTable[]` *array represents the large cabinet, while the* `MyTable0[]` *array is the top small cabinet, and* `MyTable9[]` *is the bottom small cabinet, as shown in Figure 6-3.*

If you now take all the small filing cabinets and stack them up alongside each other, you will now see how they represent the `MasterTable[]` array, as shown in Figure 6-4. To all intents and purposes we can forget about the main array (other than for using its name to index into the sub-arrays), and think only terms of the ten sub-arrays, and how to access each drawer using pairs of indexes.

The first index goes along the drawers of cabinets from left to right, and the second one goes down the drawers top to bottom. Therefore array index `[3][7]` points to the fourth filing cabinet along and the eighth drawer down.

In other words, `MasterTable[3][7]` refers to the value held in the eighth drawer down of the fourth cabinet along.

A More Practical Example

Obviously a multiplication table is a trivial thing to recreate on a computer, as it can be achieved with a couple of simple loops. So let's look instead at a more practical example: that of a board for a game of chess.

As you will know, there are 64 squares on a chess board, laid out in an 8 × 8 grid, and there are two sets of 16 pieces: black and white. Using a computer to represent a chess board in its starting position, and ignoring the fact that the squares alternate between dark and light, you might use code such as this (in which upper case letters represent white pieces, and the lower case ones are black):

```
Row0 = ['r', 'n', 'b', 'q', 'k', 'b', 'n', 'r']
Row1 = ['p', 'p', 'p', 'p', 'p', 'p', 'p', 'p']
```

```
Row2 = ['-', '-', '-', '-', '-', '-', '-', '-']
Row3 = ['-', '-', '-', '-', '-', '-', '-', '-']
Row4 = ['-', '-', '-', '-', '-', '-', '-', '-']
Row5 = ['-', '-', '-', '-', '-', '-', '-', '-']
Row6 = ['P', 'P', 'P', 'P', 'P', 'P', 'P', 'P']
Row7 = ['R', 'N', 'B', 'Q', 'K', 'B', 'N', 'R']
```

The dashes represent locations where there is no chess piece, and the key for the other letters is as follows:

- **R/r** Rooks
- **N/n** Knights
- **B/b** Bishops
- **Q/q** Queens
- **K/k** Kings
- **P/p** Pawns

You can now insert all these arrays into a master array that holds the complete chess board, like this:

```
Board = [Row0, Row1, Row2, Row3, Row4, Row5, Row6, Row7]
```

Now we are ready to move pieces about on the board. So, for example, let's assume that the white player opens with the standard *pawn to king 4* move. Using the array notation of locations `[0][0]` through `[7][7]`, with `[0][0]` being the top left corner, and `[7][7]` the bottom right, this is equivalent to setting the location `[6][4]` to `'-'` to remove the pawn currently at this location, and then setting `[4][4]` to `'P'` to place the pawn in its new position. In terms of code it would look like this:

```
Temp        = Board[6][4]
Board[6][4] = '-'
Board[4][4] = Temp
```

In this example a new variable called `Temp` is employed to store the value extracted from `Board[6][4]`. Then `Board[6][4]` is set to a dash character to remove the piece, and the value now in `Temp` is then placed into `Board[4][4]`, overwriting whatever value it previously held.

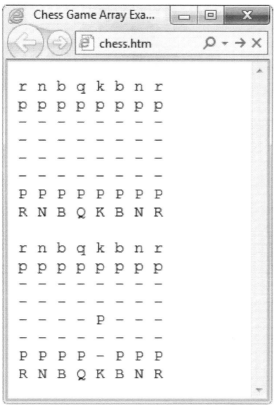

Figure 5: Modifying a two-dimensional chess board array.

Or, if it's not necessary to hold a copy of the piece being moved (which it isn't in this very simple simulation), then you can simply set the two array locations to their required values, like this:

```
Board[6][4] = '-'
Board[4][4] = 'P'
```

Figure 6-5 shows the *chess.htm* example file (available in the companion archive), in which the before and after board positions are shown, as created by the preceding code.

***Note:** If you wish you may continue adding arrays within other arrays until you run out of computer memory. All you do is place new arrays inside existing ones to add an extra dimension. For example, If you were to create an additional 8 sub-sub-arrays for each of the sub-array elements (a total of 64 new arrays), you would form eight complete chessboards in a three-dimensional array, representing an 8 × 8 × 8 cube!*

Multidimensional Associative Arrays

As you might expect, as with numeric arrays, you can create multidimensional associative arrays. Let me explain why you might want to do this by considering a small on-line store that sells toys for six different age ranges of children, as follows

- Babies
- Toddlers
- Age 3-5
- Age 5-8
- Age 8-12
- Teenagers

These categories can be easily mapped into an associative array, as I'll show you in a minute. But let's first create some sub-categories for each of the main ones, such as these:

- Babies
    - Rattle
    - Bear
    - Pacifier
- Toddlers
    - Wooden Bricks
    - Xylophone
    - Play Dough
- Age 3-5
    - Slide
    - Tricycle
    - Crayons
- Age 5-8
    - Dolly
    - Bicycle
    - Guitar
- Age 8-12
    - Tablet Computer
    - Remote Control Car
    - Frisbee
- Teenagers
    - MP3 Player
    - Game Console
    - TV/DVD Combo

Clearly these sub-categories can also be mapped to associative arrays, but before we do that we have to go even deeper (yet more undertones of *Inception*) because a web store needs things like pricing information and product availability, like this:

- Price
- Stock Level

Creating the Multi-Dimensional Array

Armed with these details we're now ready to start building the arrays needed, by assigning values to the price and stock level of each product being sold to a two-dimensional array for each product, as follows:

```
Rattle    = { 'Price' :   4.99, 'Stock' : 3 }
Bear      = { 'Price' :   6.99, 'Stock' : 2 }
Pacifier  = { 'Price' :   1.99, 'Stock' : 9 }
Bricks    = { 'Price' :   5.99, 'Stock' : 1 }
Xylophone = { 'Price' :  12.99, 'Stock' : 2 }
PlayDough = { 'Price' :   8.49, 'Stock' : 7 }
Slide     = { 'Price' :  99.99, 'Stock' : 1 }
Tricycle  = { 'Price' :  79.99, 'Stock' : 1 }
~Crayons  = { 'Price' :   3.79, 'Stock' : 5 }
Dolly     = { 'Price' :  14.99, 'Stock' : 3 }
Bicycle   = { 'Price' :  89.99, 'Stock' : 2 }
Guitar    = { 'Price' :  49.00, 'Stock' : 1 }
TabletPC  = { 'Price' : 149.99, 'Stock' : 1 }
RemoteCar = { 'Price' :  39.99, 'Stock' : 2 }
Frisbee   = { 'Price' :   7.99, 'Stock' : 6 }
MP3Player = { 'Price' : 179.99, 'Stock' : 1 }
Console   = { 'Price' : 199.99, 'Stock' : 2 }
TVAndDVD  = { 'Price' :  99.99, 'Stock' : 1 }
```

Now that these basic data structures are complete it's possible to group the products into the age range arrays, like this (where the words in quotes are the keys and those after the colons are the values, which are the names of the arrays previously created):

```
Babies    = { 'Rattle'           : Rattle,
              'Bear'             : Bear,
              'Pacifier'         : Pacifier }
Toddlers  = { 'Wooden Bricks'    : Bricks,
              'Xylophone'        : Xylophone,
              'Play Dough'       : PlayDough }
Age3_5    = { 'Slide'            : Slide,
```

```
                  'Tricycle'              : Tricycle,
                  'Crayons'               : Crayons }
   Age5_8    = { 'Dolly'                  : Dolly,
                  'Bicycle'               : Bicycle,
                  'Guitar'                : Guitar }
   Age8_12   = { 'Tablet PC'              : TabletPC,
                  'Remote Control Car'    : RemoteCar,
                  'Frisbee'               : Frisbee }
   Teenagers = { 'MP3 Player'            : MP3Player,
                  'Game Console'          : Console,
                  'TV/DVD Combo'          : TVAndDVD }
```

Note: I used an underline character between the digits in these age rage arrays since the dash is a disallowed character in variable or array names (because it can be confused with the minus symbol). The dash is acceptable, however, when used as part of a quoted string for a key name.

And finally the top array can be populated, like this (where the strings in quotes are the keys, and the values after the colons are the names of the arrays just defined):

```
   Categories = { 'Toddlers'   : Toddlers,
                   'Ages 3-5'   : Age3_5,
                   'Ages 5-8'   : Age5_8,
                   'Ages 8-12'  : Age8_12,
                   'Teenagers'  : Teenagers }
```

What has now been created is actually a three-dimensional array. The first dimension is the Categories[] array, the second is each of the age range arrays, and the third is each of the product arrays containing the price and stock level.

Note: Remember that in each of these assignments the string on the left is the key and the item on the right is the value. In all but the innermost (or lowest) case the value is the name of another array that has already been created. For the innermost case the values are numeric values: the price and stock level.

Accessing the Arrays

You can now read and write to these stored values in the following manner, which returns the price of the slide, which is 99.99 (no currency type is specified in these examples, just values):

```
   document.write(Categories['Ages 3-5']['Slide']['Price'])
```

Or, if you need to change a price on an item of inventory for any reason, such as the crayons for example (currently 3.79), you can alter it in the following manner, which reduces the price by 0.20:

```
Categories['Ages 3-5']['Crayons']['Price'] = 3.59
```

Likewise, when you sell an item of stock you can reduce the inventory level (the stock level) in a similar manner, such as the following which decreases the stock level of game consoles by 1 using the pre-decrement operator:

```
--Categories['Teenagers']['Game Console']['Stock']
```

Obviously the inventory for even the smallest on-line store is sure to be far greater than in this example, and there are going to be many additional attributes for some toys, such as different sizes and colors and even any images, descriptions, technical specifications or other details about the product that are available, all of which could easily be built into this multi-dimensional structure of arrays.

The file *toystore.htm* in the companion archive contains all the preceding pre-populated arrays and the example statements that access them. You may wish to try experimenting with it to read from and write to other items of data within the array structure.

Note: The actual job of storing all your data will take place on a web server in a secure environment tightly controlled by your database management system. The purpose of using a structure of arrays in JavaScript like this, therefore, is purely for you to support easy manipulation of data for users within their browsers as they view your merchandise, without them having to leave your page, or transfer any data to or from the web server until an item is added to the user's shopping basket.

Summary

You should be starting to see why I called this a Crash Course because we've now covered a huge amount of territory in just 6 lectures. Hopefully, though, it's all making sense to you, and arrays are beginning to feel like second nature. Therefore, in the next lecture we'll look at some fun we can have using the array accessing functions provided with JavaScript.

THE JAVASCRIPT ARRAY FUNCTIONS

By studying the contents this lecture you will:

- ✓ *Learn all the most useful array handling functions.*
- ✓ *Be able to join and split arrays to and from each other.*
- ✓ *Know how to map functions to array elements.*

TO MAKE ARRAYS even more powerful, JavaScript comes ready-made with a selection of handy functions for accessing and manipulating arrays. For example you can join arrays together, push new items into an array (and pop them off again later), reverse the data in an array, sort it alphabetically or numerically, and more.

So, in this lecture, we'll look at these functions and how to use them.

Using for(... in ...)

The first feature I'd like to introduce is for(... in ...), because with it you can iterate through an array one element at a time, which we will need to do in the following examples in order to see the results. To show how this iteration works let's start with a simple array:

```
Cats = [ 'Long Hair',
         'Short Hair',
         'Dwarf',
         'Farm',
         'Tabby',
         'Tortoiseshell' ]
```

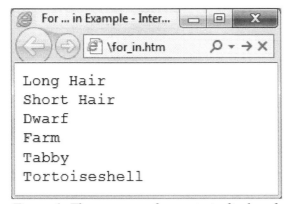

Figure 1: The contents of Cats() *is displayed.*

Now, let's use for (... in ...) to display all its elements, as follows (resulting in Figure 7-1):

```
for (index in Cats)
{
    document.write(Cats[index] + '<br />')
}
```

What's happening here is the for() keyword creates a new variable called index, which it initializes with the integer value of 0, so that it points to the first element in the array specified (in this case Cats[]).

Then the contents of the curly braces is executed once for each element in the Cats[] array, with index being incremented each time around. So the first time element 0 is indexed by index, the second time it is element 1, and so on until there are no more elements left in the array to process.

For reasons I will explain in Lecture 11 the curly braces can be omitted when there is only a single statement to be executed by such a for() loop. Therefore, for the sake of simplicity in the following examples, I will reduce this type of code to the much shorter following example, which also uses the index variable i instead of index, but is equally valid syntax:

```
for (i in Cats) document.write(Cats[i] + '<br />')
```

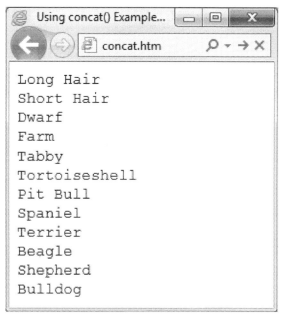

Figure 2: The two arrays have been concatenated.

Now that there's an easy way to display the contents of an array, we can start to look at the array functions provided by JavaScript, and see how to use them. You can try this example for yourself by loading the *for_in.htm* example from the companion archive into your browser.

Using `concat()`

Using the `concat()` function you can return a new array created by joining two other arrays together. The two original arrays are not changed in any way by this function, only the result of joining them together is returned.

To see how this works let's create a second array to go with the `Cats[]` array created a little earlier, as follows:

```
Dogs = [ 'Pit Bull',
         'Spaniel',
         'Terrier',
         'Beagle',
         'Shepherd',
         'Bulldog' ]
```

With both arrays now created we can now run the `concat()` function on them, like this:

```
Pets = Cats.concat(Dogs)
```

And now to see the result of this operation we can issue the following statement:

```
for (i in Pets) document.write(Pets[i] + '<br />')
```

The code to create these two arrays and the preceding pair of statements are in the *concat.htm* file in the companion archive. As you can see in Figure 7-2 the result is that the new array `Pets[]` now contains all elements from both the `Cats[]` and `Dogs[]` arrays, in order.

For a similar result, but with the contents of the `Dogs[]` array before the `Cats[]`, you could equally have issued this statement:

```
Pets = Dogs.concat(Cats)
```

In fact, you could omit the creation of the `Pets[]` array altogether and simply iterate through the result of the `concat()` call, like this:

```
for (i in Dogs.concat(Cats))
    document.write(Dogs.concat(Cats)[i] + '<br />')
```

Note: Although it works, the preceding is wasteful code since the `concat()` function has ended up being called twice, because in this example the result of the concatenation is lost once you have accessed it, so it's not recommended coding practice. However this code does illustrate that by placing square brackets containing an index variable after the call to `concat()` (namely `[i]`), you can index into the array returned by the call.

An Alternative to `concat()`

By the way, if all you want to do is quickly see what values are in an array, you can use the implied concatenation you get when referencing an array as an argument to the `document.write()` function. For example, you can list all the elements in the `Dogs[]` array to the browser (separated with commas) like this:

```
document.write(Dogs)
```

Figure 3: The result of joining array elements into a string.

Note how you must omit the `[]` characters from after the array name in order for this to work, and the result of this statement will then be like the following:

Pit Bull,Spaniel,Terrier,Beagle,Shepherd,Bulldog

Using `join()`

Sometimes you may wish to turn all the elements in an array into a string, and this is easy to do using the `join()` function. For example, let's take the case of the `Cats[]` array, as follows:

```
document.write(Cats.join(' and '))
```

This statement calls the `join()` function, passing it the string `' and '`, which is used as a separator, which is inserted between each element, as shown in Figure 7-3.

You may use any string as the element separator, or none at all, as in the following three examples (with extra spaces inserted to clearly show what's going on):

```
document.write(Cats.join(', ') + '<br />')
document.write(Cats.join(''  ) + '<br />')
document.write(Cats.join( )  )
```

When no argument is passed to `join()` a comma is assumed as the separator, while to have no separator you should supply an empty string (`''`). So, in turn, the three previous statements display the following:

Long Hair, Short Hair, Dwarf, Farm, Tabby, Tortoiseshell
Long HairShort HairDwarfFarmTabbyTortoiseshell
Long Hair,Short Hair,Dwarf,Farm,Tabby,Tortoiseshell

The `forEach()` Function

An alternative to using `for(… in …)` is the `forEach()` function. With it you can iterate through an array of elements very easily, as follows (where `v` in the arguments of the `Info()` function is the value of each element, `i` is the index of the element, and `a` is the array contents):

```
Dogs = [ 'Pit Bull',
         'Spaniel',
         'Terrier',
         'Beagle',
         'Shepherd',
         'Bulldog' ]

Dogs.forEach(Info)

function Info(v, i, a)
{
   document.write('[' + i + '] is ' + v + '<br />')
}
```

As shown in Figure 7-4, the `Info()` function simply displays information about each element in the array. The powerful thing is that the `forEach` function name is simply attached to the `Dogs` array name with a period operator and (without needing any loops) the array gets processed by the `Info()` function, which has been passed as the argument to `forEach()`.

The `map()` function

One very quick and easy way to process all the elements in an array is to pass the array to a function, via JavaScript's `map()` function. For example, the following code creates an array populated with numbers, and then applies the `Math.sqrt()` function to each element, returning the results in the new array `Roots`, all via a single call to the `maps()` function.

```
Nums  = [99, 16, 11, 66.5, 54, 23]
Roots = Nums.map(Math.sqrt)
```

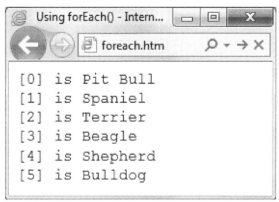

Figure 4: Iterating through an array with forEach().

You can see the result of running this code (*maps.htm* in the companion archive) in Figure 7-5.

Using push ()

There are a couple of good reasons for using the push() function. Firstly you can add a new element to the end of an array without knowing how many items already exist in that array. For example, normally you would need to know the current array length and then use that value to add extra values, like this (using the Cats[] array once more):

```
Cats = [ 'Long Hair',
         'Short Hair',
         'Dwarf',
         'Farm',
         'Tabby',
         'Tortoiseshell' ]

len       = Cats.length
Cats[len] = "Siamese"
```

The new variable len is used to hold the length of the array (the number of elements it contains). In this instance the value will be 6, for element 0 through 5. Therefore the value in len, being 6, is suitable to use as an index into the next available element, and so that is what it is used for – the value 6 pointing to the seventh element, since element indexes start at 0.

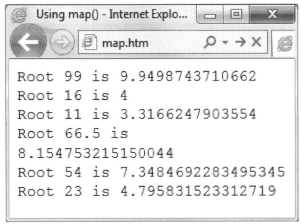

Figure 5: Applying the map() function to an array.

In fact, if the variable `len` is not to be used anywhere else it's actually superfluous, so you could replace the final two lines of the preceding example with this single statement:

```
Cats[Cats.length] = "Siamese"
```

However, it is much simpler to let JavaScript keep track of array lengths and simply tell it to add a new element to the `cats[]` array, like this:

```
Cats.push('Siamese')
```

You can verify that the element has been added with the following `for()` loop (which results in Figure 7-6, the code for which is available as *push.htm* in the companion archive):

```
for (i in Cats) document.write(Cats[i] + '<br />')
```

The second reason you might want to use `Push()` is because it's a quick way of storing values in a sequence that then have to be recalled in the reverse order. For example, using `push()` you can keep adding elements to an array, like this:

```
MyArray.push('A')
MyArray.push('B')
MyArray.push('C')
```

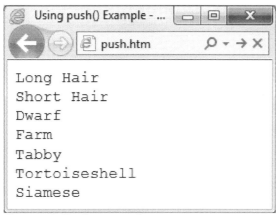
Figure 6: Pushing an element onto an array.

Then, as you will see in the following description of pop(), you can also remove these elements from last to first, such that the value 'C' will be taken of first, then 'B', then 'A', and so on.

Using pop()

At its simplest pop() enables you to remove the last element from an array (and in this instance discard the returned value), using code such as this:

```
MyArray.pop()
```

Or, to remove the last element from an array and store it in a variable (for example), you use code such as this:

```
MyVariable = MyArray.pop()
```

You can apply pop() to an existing array with values in, which can have been assigned when the array was created, via a call to push() or in any other way. The pop() function then pulls the last item off the array (removing it from the array) and then returns that value. Looking again at the Cats[] array, a working example might look like this:

```
Cats = [ 'Long Hair',
         'Short Hair',
         'Dwarf',
         'Farm',
         'Tabby',
         'Tortoiseshell' ]
```

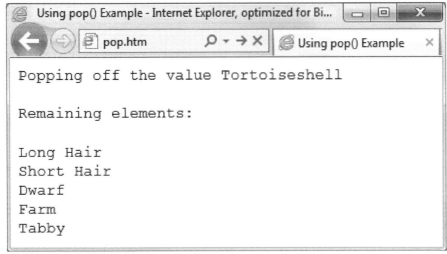

Figure 7: Popping an element off an array.

```
document.write('Popping off the value ' +
    Cats.pop() + '<br /><br />')

document.write('Remaining elements: <br /><br />')
for (i in Cats) document.write(Cats[i] + '<br />')
```

The result of running this code (available as *pop.htm* in the companion archive) is shown in Figure 7-7, where you can see that the value 'Tortoiseshell' was popped off the array, and underneath all the remaining elements are displayed, confirming that the previous final element has now been removed.

Using push() and pop() Together

The pop() function is most commonly used with push() when writing code that uses recursion. Recursion is any section of code that calls itself, and which can then call itself again, and keep on doing so until the task of the code is complete (it's like *Inception* yet again!).

If this sounds complicated consider a search algorithm for exploring a maze such as the one in Figure 7-8, in which the objective is to find your way from the starting point at a to the finish at y.

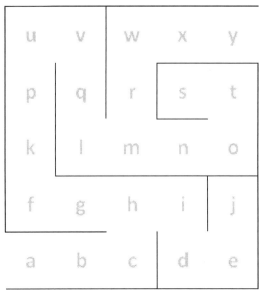

Figure 8: A simple 5 × 5 maze.

You can clearly see the path to follow, but a computer is not so smart and will need to investigate the maze as if it's a rat, with walls higher than it can see over. Therefore a program to do this will easily find its way along the path a-b-c-h, but then it will encounter a choice of going either left to location (or cell) g, or right to i.

Let's assume it chooses the latter after selecting a direction at random. The program will then follow the path i-d-e-j, only to encounter a dead end, requiring the program to return. Let's look at tracking this entire path so far using the push() function:

```
Maze = new Array()
Maze.push('a')
Maze.push('b')
Maze.push('c')
Maze.push('h')
Maze.push('i')
Maze.push('d')
Maze.push('e')
Maze.push('j')
```

If you assume that there's also some extra code (not documented here) that knows which cells it has and hasn't yet visited, the program can now use the simple method of popping each cell off the array until it reaches one where it can get to a cell not yet visited. Pseudo-code (the actions to take expressed in plain English) to do this might look as follows:

```
While no unvisited cell is accessible
   pop a location off the array
```

And the sequence of actions that would happen within the loop section of this code would be like this:

```
Location = Maze.pop() // Returns 'j'
```

Since no unvisited cell can be reached from 'j' (as determined by the code that we assume is there but not documented) the loop will go round again, and again, until an unvisited cell can be accessed, resulting in four additional calls to pop(), as follows:

```
Location = Maze.pop() // Returns 'e'
Location = Maze.pop() // Returns 'd'
Location = Maze.pop() // Returns 'i'
Location = Maze.pop() // Returns 'h'
```

Now, when the program finds it has popped the location 'h' off the stack, it discovers there's a new cell it can go to, namely 'g', and so the process continues along the path g-f-k-p-u-v-q-l-m, at which point another choice of directions is encountered: either 'r' or 'n'.

To track this path the program will push all the cells between 'g' and 'm' onto the array, and then also push the path n-o-t-s, at which point another dead end is encountered.

Then, as before, the code pops off all the cells in a loop until it reaches 'm', at which point the unvisited cell 'r' is accessible and the final path out of the maze is discovered: r-w-x-y.

Note: Recursion is quite complex programming, especially for beginners, which is why I have not documented the ancillary code you would use to take care of tracking the visited and unvisited cells. I simply wanted to offer a visual example of recursion that would explain what's going on, and show how to use push() and pop() together. But don't worry if you find any of it confusing, as you can safely move on with the course and come back here another time, when you find an actual need for these functions.

Figure 9: Array elements before and after reversing.

Using `reverse()`

When you want to reverse the order of elements in an array you can call the `reverse()` function, which actually reverses the array contents, rather than returning a new array as some other functions do.

To use the function simply attach it to the array to be reversed, like this:

```
MyArray.reverse()
```

Figure 7-9 shows this function being used to reverse the `Cats[]` array from previous examples, the code for which is available as *reverse.htm* in the companion archive.

Using FILO and FIFO Arrays

The `reverse()` function is sometimes used on an array of elements that have been created by popping the values onto it. As you will know from the earlier `push()` section, pushed values are added to the end of an array such that when you come to pop them off again they are returned in reverse order. This is often referred to as a FILO (First In / Last Out) array. When an array is used this way it is also sometimes called a *stack*.

But if you wish to operate a FIFO (First In / First Out) stack, you can reverse an array before pushing an item onto it and then reverse it again ready for elements to be popped off. That way the first value pushed onto it will be the first one popped off, and so on.

This type of array or stack is also known as a *buffer*, and is typically used for handling events such as keyboard input, in which the key presses should be stored (buffered) until needed, and returned in the order they were pressed.

Buffering Using an Array

You can see a simulation of this in the following code, in which the word `'Fred'` is being pushed into the array `Buffer()`, with the array's contents shown in the comment immediately following each statement. The top (or start) of the array is at the left of the string shown in the comments, and the bottom (or end) of the array (onto which values are pushed and popped) is at the right of the string:

```
Buffer.reverse() // Buffer = ''
Buffer.push('F') // Buffer = 'F'
Buffer.reverse() // Buffer = 'F'

Buffer.reverse() // Buffer = 'F'
Buffer.push('r') // Buffer = 'Fr'
Buffer.reverse() // Buffer = 'rF'

Buffer.reverse() // Buffer = 'Fr'
Buffer.push('e') // Buffer = 'Fre'
Buffer.reverse() // Buffer = 'erF'

Buffer.reverse() // Buffer = 'Fre'
Buffer.push('d') // Buffer = 'Fred'
Buffer.reverse() // Buffer = 'derF'
```

Initially `Buffer()` is empty and has no elements, but then the letter `'F'` is pushed onto it. Seeing as the array has only a single element, reversing it at this point has no effect. However, when the next letter, `'r'`, is to be added it is pushed to the bottom of the array, denoted in the comment as being on the right of the `'F'`.

After reversing the array back again the `'r'` is at the top and `'F'` is at the bottom of the array. This is exactly where we want them because if the code that uses this buffering system is ready to process the next key press in the buffer, it can simply issue a call to `pop()`, which will pull the letter `'F'` off it. This is correct because when processing buffered data such as this, the letters typed must be processed in the order typed.

When the letter `'e'` is processed the array is once again reversed so that it can be added to the bottom of the array, then the array is reversed back again so that should pop() be called at *this* point, `'F'` will be the first letter popped off. After this third set of statements `'F'` is at the bottom of the array, `'r'` is in the middle, and `'e'` is at the top.

Finally the letter `'d'` is processed using the same procedure so that after it has been placed in the array it is at the top, with the `'F'` at the bottom.

A Sneak Peak at Writing Functions

If you need a way to push values to the start of an array (instead of the end) you can create a `PushToTop()` function, using `push()` in conjunction with `reverse()`:

```
function PushToTop(AnArray, value)
{
  AnArray.reverse()
  AnArray.push(value)
  AnArray.reverse()
}
```

Then you simply call the new function, instead of each group of three statements in the previous example, like this:

```
PushToTop(Buffer, 'F')
PushToTop(Buffer, 'r')
PushToTop(Buffer, 'e')
PushToTop(Buffer, 'd')
```

Actually, JavaScript *does* have an in-built function to do this – I simply wanted to show how you could combine `reverse()` and `push()` to achieve the same result. But you can, in fact, 'push' values to the top of an array using the (curiously named) `unshift()` function. Likewise you can 'pop' from the top of an array using the `shift()` function.

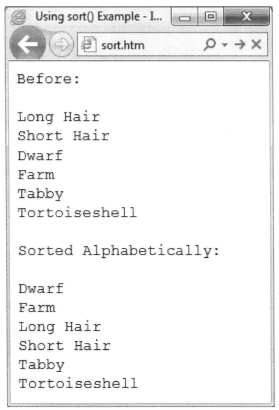

Figure 10: Sorting an array alphabetically.

Note: *But let's not get too far ahead of ourselves quite yet, as there are a couple more array functions to introduce, before getting to creating your own functions in the following Lecture.*

Using `sort()`

JavaScript comes with a handy `sort()` function to sort arrays alphabetically in ascending order. This function changes the actual array to which it is applied, unlike some other functions that simply return a new array, leaving the original untouched.

To sort an array simply attach the `sort()` function to the array, as with this example that uses the `Cats[]` array:

```
Cats = [ 'Long Hair',
         'Short Hair',
```

```
                        'Dwarf',
                        'Farm',
                        'Tabby',
                        'Tortoiseshell' ]

    Cats.sort()
```

The result of issuing this `sort()` call (the code for which is available as *sort.htm* in the companion archive) is shown in Figure 7-10.

Tailoring the `sort()` Function

If all you require is an alphabetical sort in ascending order then `sort()` is just the function for you. However, should you need to sort in reverse order or sort an array numerically then you need to provide some extra code to `sort()` to help it achieve this.

Note: Enhancing the `sort()` function requires using functions that you will write, so because I won't properly cover functions until the Lecture 10, if the following makes you scratch your head, remember that you can simply copy and paste the code and it will work anyway, without you having to know (yet) just how it works.

Sorting Numerically

In order to sort an array numerically you must pass a helper function to the `sort()` function. This helper needs to tell `sort()` how to compare pairs of items as it sorts. So, to sort an array numerically you can supply a function such as this:

```
    function SortNumeric(a, b)
    {
      return a - b
    }
```

What this function does is accept two array elements (for example it might be element 0 and element 1) and then it tests whether the first element is greater than the second by subtracting the second from the first.

If the result of this subtraction is greater than 0, then b is smaller than a. Or, if it's less than 0, then b is greater than a, otherwise they have the same value. So what gets returned by `SortNumeric()` is either a negative, a zero or a positive value, from which the `sort()` function decides the order in which to place the two elements, as follows:

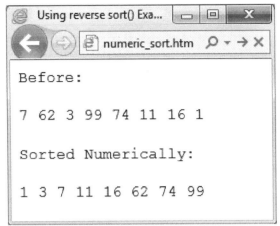

Figure 11: Sorting an array numerically.

- If the result returned by SortNumeric() is negative, then b is greater than a and therefore the element represented by a must appear before the one represented by b.
- If the result is positive then b is smaller than a and so the element represented by b must appear before that represented by a.
- If the values in a and b are equal there is no need to change the positions of the elements represented by a and b, so nothing happens.

The SortNumeric() function is passed to the sort() function, like this:

```
Numbers = [7, 62, 3, 99, 74, 11, 16, 1]
Numbers.sort(SortNumeric)
```

The first statement creates the array Numbers[], in which a variety of different numeric values are stored. Then the second statement calls the sort() function on that array, passing it the name of the helper function to use (namely SortNumeric), but omitting the round brackets that usually follow a function name.

This is because we are telling sort() which function to use, and not passing it the result of calling the function (more on this in the following lecture).

The result of running this code is shown in Figure 7-11.

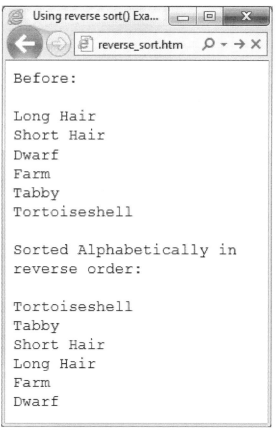

Figure 12: Reversing a sorted array.

Reversing a Sort

To obtain a reversed sort of any kind all you need to do is pass the sorted array to the `reverse()` function, like this (as shown in Figure 7-12):

```
Cats.sort().reverse()
```

Note: You will probably have realized that for numeric arrays the expression `return a - b` *in the* `SortNumeric()` *function could be replaced with* `return b - a`, *which would also result in a reversed sort – one example of how you can achieve the same outcome in JavaScript using different methods.*

Using `splice()`

I've left possibly the most powerful array function, `splice()`, until last – not just because it comes last alphabetically, but because you can use it to provide the same facility as most of the other array functions, and a lot more too.

With `splice()` you can remove one or more elements from an array, or insert one or more into an array, and you can do either at any position within the array. What's more, you can remove and insert at the same time, providing a replace facility that can swap one or more elements with more, the same or fewer elements.

Removing Elements From an Array

Let's look first at how to remove one or more elements from an array, starting with the `Cats[]` array we've been using a lot. In the following example the `splice()` function is called with two arguments. The first is the element at which to perform the splice (starting from 0), and the second is the number of elements to be removed:

```
Cats = [ 'Long Hair',
         'Short Hair',
         'Dwarf',
         'Farm',
         'Tabby',
         'Tortoiseshell' ]

Cats.splice(2, 3)
```

Therefore, with arguments of 2 and 3, the splice starts at the element index 2, which is the third one, and the second argument of 3 states that three elements are to be removed from the array. If you need to know which elements have been removed you can access the result of calling the function, which is an array containing the removed elements, like this:

```
Removed = Cats.splice(2, 3)
```

Figure 7-13 shows this code brought together, displaying the array before splicing, the elements removed by the splice, and the elements remaining afterwards.

Figure 13: Removing elements from an array.

Inserting Elements Into an Array

Using a similar call to splice() you can insert new values into the array, as in the following example, which adds two more breeds of cat starting at the third element:

```
Cats.splice(2, 0, 'Siamese', 'Persian')
```

Here, the first argument of two is the third element in the array, and the second argument of 0 tells splice() there are no elements to be removed. After this there are two new arguments, which tell splice() to insert them into the array starting at element 2 (the third one). You may place as many values as you like here to insert as many new elements as you need. The result of making this call is shown in Figure 7-14.

Figure 14: Inserting values into an array.

Advanced Array Splicing

Finally, you can remove and insert elements at the same time using a call such as the following:

```
Cats.splice(2, 3, 'Siamese', 'Persian')
```

This statement tells `splice()` to use a splice index of 2 (the third element), at which location it must remove three elements, and then insert the new values supplied. The result of issuing this call is shown in Figure 7-15.

Figure 15: Removing from and inserting items into an array.

Example files are available in the companion archive demonstrating all three types of splicing. They are *splice.htm, insert_splice.htm* and *advanced_splice.htm*.

Summary

You now know how to use all types of JavaScript array, whether single or multi-dimensional, numeric, string, associative or otherwise. Coupled with your earlier knowledge of variables and operators you are now ready to really get down to power programming, beginning with the following lecture on controlling program flow.

CONTROLLING PROGRAM FLOW

By following this lecture you will:

- ✓ *Learn how to change the flow of program execution..*
- ✓ *Understand how to use conditional statements.*
- ✓ *Know how to best handle long lists of options.*

HAVING REACHED THIS point in the course you've actually already learned the vast majority of JavaScript. You should understand how to incorporate it into a web page, the syntax to use, handling numeric variables, strings and arrays, using operators in expressions according to their associativity, and you've even learned the basics of handling program flow control using the `if()` and `else` keywords.

In this lecture you'll consolidate your knowledge of the latter so that you can precisely control the flow of program execution.

The `if()` Statement

You've already seen this statement in use a few times, but only with single line statements, so here's the full syntax of an `if()` statement:

```
if (expression)
{
  // Execute this code, which can be one...
  // ...or more lines
}
```

In this example expression can be any expression at all created using numbers, strings, variables, objects and operators. The result of the expression must be a Boolean value that can be either `true` or `false`, such as `if (MyVar > 7)` ..., and so on.

The curly braces encapsulate the code that must be executed upon the expression evaluating to `true`, and there can be none, one, or many statements.

Omitting the Braces

To enable you to create short and simple `if()` statements without having to use braces, they are optional if only one statement is to be executed upon the expression being `true`, like this:

```
if (Time < 12) document.write('Good morning')
```

If the code to execute is quite long (so that it might wrap to the following line) you may wish to start it on the following line, but if you do so, because no curly braces are being used to encapsulate the statement, it's best to indent the statement by a few spaces or a tab, so that it clearly belongs to the `if()` statement, like this:

```
if (Time < 12)
    document.write('Good morning. How are you today?')
```

Indeed, if you have a really long statement to execute it can also be a good idea to split it over several lines at suitable points, like this:

```
if (Time < 12)
    document.write('Good morning. Following is the " +
        'list of all your appointments for today. The " +
        'important' ones are highlighted in bold')
```

Here I have split the output into three parts by breaking it into three strings, which are displayed one after the other using + operators. I also further indented the follow on lines to clearly indicate that they belong to the `document.write()` call.

However, in my view this has become a borderline case where you might be better advised to encapsulate the statement within curly braces, because they will ensure there is no ambiguity, and you won't have worry about the wrapping of long lines diminishing the code readability, like this:

```
if (Time < 12)
{
   document.write('Good morning. Following is the list of all
your appointments for today. The important ones are
highlighted in bold')
}
```

Some program editors will automatically indent wrapped around lines for you (based on the indent at the start of the line) making the code even more readable, and looking like this:

```
if (Time < 12)
{
   document.write('Good morning. Following is the list of
   all your appointments for today. The important ones are
   chighlighted in bold')
}
```

Note: *In this latter case, the program editor will treat all three lines of the statement as a single line, which they are. Don't try to format your code like this using newlines, though, as it will split it into multiple lines and cause errors – unless you also break the statement into parts, as detailed earlier.*

Positioning of Braces

The reason you can lay out your code in a variety of ways is that JavaScript supports the use of tabs, spaces and newlines as *whitespace*, which is ignored (other than newlines placed within a statement which indicate a statement end, and can be avoided only by splitting statements into parts).

Because of this programmers can choose to place the curly braces wherever they like. As you have seen, when I use them I generally place the opening and closing brace directly under the if() statement's first character, and then indent the encapsulated statements, like this:

```
if (expression)
{
   // Execute this code, which can be one...
   // ...or more lines
}
```

Other programmers, however, choose to place the opening curly brace immediately after the if(), like this:

```
if (expression) {
  // Execute this code, which can be one...
  // ...or more lines
}
```

Both of these (and other) types of layout (such as leaving the closing curly brace at the end of the final statement) are perfectly acceptable.

Note: There are also some less-used layouts used by other programmers, but the preceding tend to be the main two. I advocate the first type because (even though it requires an extra line of code for each opening brace) it makes the opening braces indent to the level of the closing ones, so that if you have several nested statements, you can more clearly determine that you have the right number of opening and closing braces, and that they are all in the right places. It also places more vertical whitespace between the expression and the statements that follow, which I find helpful. However, which system you use is entirely up to you.

The `else` Statement

To accompany the `if()` statement there's also an `else` keyword, which follows the same rules as `if()`, except the code following an `else` is executed only if the expression following the `if()` evaluates to `false`.

If the code comprises a single statement it doesn't require encapsulating in curly braces, but if it has two or more statements braces are required.

You use the `else` keyword in conjunction with `if()`, like this:

```
if (Age < 18)
{
  document.write('You are not an adult.')
}
else
{
  document.write('You are an adult.')
}
```

Since both of these keywords only include a single statement you can safely omit the braces if you wish, like this:

```
if (Age < 18)
   document.write('You are not an adult.')
else
   document.write('You are an adult.')
```

Or, if there's room, you can even move the statements up to directly follow the keywords, like this:

```
if (Age < 18) document.write('You are not an adult.')
else          document.write('You are an adult.')
```

Note: In this instance I opted to indent the second statement until it lined up underneath the first one. This helps make it clear what's going on at a glance if I were to come back to this code some months later. However, how you lay out your whitespace is entirely up to you.

There is another convention regarding braces that I recommend you consider using, which is that if one of the statements in an `if()` ... `else` construct uses braces, then so should the other, even if the other one only has a single statement. You can see the difference in the following (all valid) examples, in which I think you'll find that Example 3 (with both sets of statements in braces) is the easiest to follow:

```
if (Age < 18) // Example 1
{
   document.write('You are not an adult. ')
   document.write('Sorry, you cannot vote yet.')
}
else
   document.write('You are an adult.')

if (Age < 18) // Example 2
   document.write('You are not an adult. ')
else
{
   document.write('You are an adult. ')
   document.write('You can vote.')
}

if (Age < 18) // Example 3
{
```

```
    document.write('You are not an adult. ')
    document.write('Sorry, you cannot vote yet.')
  }
  else
  {
    document.write('You are an adult.')
  }
```

You don't *have* to follow this advice, but it will certainly make your debugging a lot easier if you do, and any other programmers who have to maintain your code will thank you for it.

The `else if()` statement

You can extend the power of `if()` ... `else` even further by also incorporating `else if()` statements, which provide a third option to the original `if()` statement, and which you place before the final `else` statement (if there is one).

The following example illustrates how you might use this keyword:

```
if (Value < 0)       document.write('Negative')
else if (Value > 0)  document.write('Positive')
else                 document.write('Zero')
```

Note: As with other examples, I have used whitespace liberally in the preceding code to line the statements up and make them easier to follow.

The `else if()` statement follows the same rules as the `if()` and `else` statements with regard to using curly braces to encapsulate multiple statements (but not requiring them for single statements). However I give the same recommendation as I did earlier that if even one of the parts of an `if()` ... `else if()` ... `else` structure uses braces, then I advise you to use braces for all parts.

Of course, you don't have to use a concluding `else` after an `if()` ... `else if()` construct if you don't want it. For example, if you don't need to deal with the case of a zero value (perhaps because one is not possible in the code you have written), you might simply use the following:

```
if (Value < 0)       document.write('Negative')
else if (Value > 0)  document.write('Positive')
```

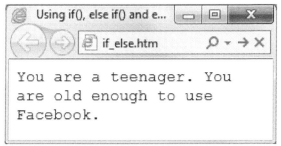

Figure 1: Using multiple else if() *statements.*

Note: *The purpose of the* else *keyword is as a catch-all, to trap all possible values that remain and execute the statement(s) attached to it if none of the preceding statements in the clause are* true.

The switch() Statement

The if(), else if() and else statements are very powerful, and comprise much of JavaScript programming. But they are not the most efficient method of controlling program flow when there are more than three options to consider. For example, imagine there's an input field on the web page with the following string values from which the user must select their age range:

- 0-1
- 2-3
- 4-6
- 7-12
- 13-17
- 18+

Now here's some code you might use to process the value returned by the input, as shown in Figure 8-1 in which a value of '13-17' has been pre-selected for the string variable Age (using the *if_else.htm* file from the companion archive):

```
if (Age == '0-1')
{
   document.write('You are a baby. ')
   document.write('How can you read this?')
}
else if (Age == '2-3')
```

```
{
  document.write('You are a toddler.')
}
else if (Age == '4-6')
{
  document.write('You are an infant. ')
  document.write('You go to nursery or school.')
}
else if (Age == '7-12')
{
  document.write('You are a child.')
}
else if (Age == '13-17')
{
  document.write('You are a teenager. ')
  document.write('You can use Facebook.')
}
else document.write('You are an adult.')
```

Don't you think all those repeated else if() statement are rather cumbersome, and the code feels somewhat heavier than it could be?

Well the answer is to restructure code such as this using a switch() statement in conjunction with the case and break keywords, like this (as shown in Figure 8-2, created using the *switch.htm* file from the companion archive, and in which the string Age is pre-assigned the value '4-6'):

```
switch(Age)
{
  case '0-1':    document.write('You are a baby. ')
                 document.write('How can you read this?')
                 break
  case '2-3':    document.write('You are a toddler.')
                 break
  case '4-6':    document.write('You are an infant. ')
                 document.write('You go to school now.')
                 break
  case '7-12':   document.write('You are a child.')
                 break
  case '13-17':  document.write('You are a teenager. ')
                 document.write('You can use Facebook.')
  default:       document.write('You are an adult.')
}
```

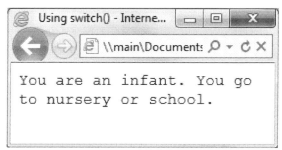

Figure 2: Using a `switch()` *statement.*

I'm sure you'll agree that using `switch()` statements is a lot clearer than a set of sprawling `else if()`s. To use one simply place the expression or variable to be tested in the brackets following the `switch` keyword, then within a pair of curly braces (which are required), provide a number of `case` statements and an optional `default` statement.

Following each `case` keyword place one possible value that the `switch` variable or expression might have. In this example `Age` can only have string values, but you can equally test for digits or floating point numbers too. After the possible value place a colon followed by the statements to execute if the value matches the `switch` variable or expression. In this example it's one or more `document.write()` statements.

Note: Note how no curly braces are required to contain multiple statements. This is because, once the code following the colon starts executing, it will keep on going, executing statement after statement (ignoring the `case` *tests), until the closing curly brace at the end of the* `switch()` *statement is encountered.*

Using the **break** Keyword

Because program flow will continue to the end of a `switch()` statement (executing all the remaining statements regardless of any `case` keywords encountered) you must mark the end of a sequence of statements to be executed with a `break` keyword. This causes program flow to jump to just after the closing brace of the `switch()` statement.

Note: You will also encounter the `break` *keyword in Lecture 9 where it is used to break to the end of looping structures of code.*

Using the `default` Keyword

In the same way that the `else` keyword is a catch-all device for dealing with any other values not caught by `if()` or `else if()` statements, you can use the `default` keyword within a `switch()` statement to catch any values not matched by the `case` statements.

In the previous example, since all possible values for `Age` are tested for except for `'18+'`, then if none of the case statements match, `Age` must contain the value `'18+'`. Therefore the `default` statement is triggered and the statement following it writes the string `'You are an adult.'` to the browser.

Note: There is no `break` keyword after the `default` option in the preceding example because it is the last statement in the `switch()` statement, and therefore a `break` keyword is superfluous in this position, as it would only add extra, unnecessary code. There is, however, nothing stopping you placing the `default` statement anywhere within a `switch()` statement (even at the start), but if you do so you must add a `break` keyword after the statements it executes, or program flow will fall through to the following statements, rather than to the end of the `switch()` statement.

Allowing Fall-through

Sometimes you may not want to use the `break` keyword because you wish to allow cases to fall-through to other cases. For example, consider the case of wanting to choose the correct language to display on a multi-national website. Using a simple input field (or even a geolocation program if you want to be really smart) you could return a string containing the user's country name, for example, perhaps out of the following:

- `Australia`
- `Brazil`
- `France`
- `Germany`
- `Portugal`
- `Spain`
- `UK`
- `USA`

Then code to process the country name in the variable `Country` to a language to use in the variable `Language` might look like this:

```
switch(Country)
{
  case 'Australia':
  case 'UK':
  case 'USA':
  default:        Language = 'English'
                  break
  case 'Brazil':
  case 'Portugal': Language = 'Portuguese'
                  break
  case 'France':  Language = 'French'
                  break
  case 'Germany': Language = 'German'
                  break
  case 'Spain':   Language = 'Spanish'
}
```

Only after the variable `Language` has been assigned its value is the `break` keyword used. So if any of the countries `'Australia'`, `'UK'` or `'USA'` are selected, then `Language` is set to `'English'`, which is also selected (because the `default` keyword is included within the fall-through group of cases) for any other value not tested for by the cases in the `switch()` statement.

A fall-through also occurs for `'Brazil'` and `'Portugal'`, both of which countries speak `'Portuguese'`, but the remaining countries have different languages and don't use any `case` fall-throughs. Note that there is no `break` keyword after the final statement as it is not needed because the end of the `switch()` has already been reached.

Note: Yes I know that many people in the USA speak Spanish, but this is simply an example to explain fall-through. If you wanted to cater for that option, though, you could have two country names for the USA: `'USA English'` and `'USA Spanish'`, and then simply add a fall-through to the `'Spain'` case – while you are at it you could also add `'Canada English'` and `'Canada French'` in a similar fashion to cater for its two languages, and so on.

Summary

This lecture concludes everything you need to know to write basic JavaScript programs. You can now handle data in various ways, including variables and arrays, you are able to use complex operators and expressions, and now you can direct the flow of your programs. In the next Lecture, therefore, we'll start to look at more advanced aspects of JavaScript, beginning with putting together various types of looping constructs.

LOOPING SECTIONS OF CODE

By following this lecture you will:

- ✓ *Learn the power of using loops for repetitive tasks.*
- ✓ *Discover the different types of loop structures available.*
- ✓ *Know how to break out of a loop when necessary.*

IN THE PREVIOUS lecture you learned all about program flow control, branching, and using `if()`, `else` and `switch()` statements. These are perfect for altering the program flow according to values and expressions, but not so good when you need to repetitively execute a process, such as processing a document a word at a time to find typographical errors.

This is the type of situation where JavaScript's looping statements come into their own. With them you form a loop around a core group of statements and then keep the loop circulating until (or unless) one or more conditions are met such as (in the case of a spelling checker) when the end of the document is reached.

More than that, the different loop types supported also enable you to pre-assign values to variables used in the loop, or only enter into a loop if a certain expression is satisfied.

Using `while()` Loops

The `while()` statement provides the simplest type of JavaScript loop. In English what it does is something like this: "While such-and-such is true then keep doing so-and-so until such-and-such is no-longer true, or forever if such-and-such is never true". Here's an example that will display the ten times table (as shown in Figure 9-1):

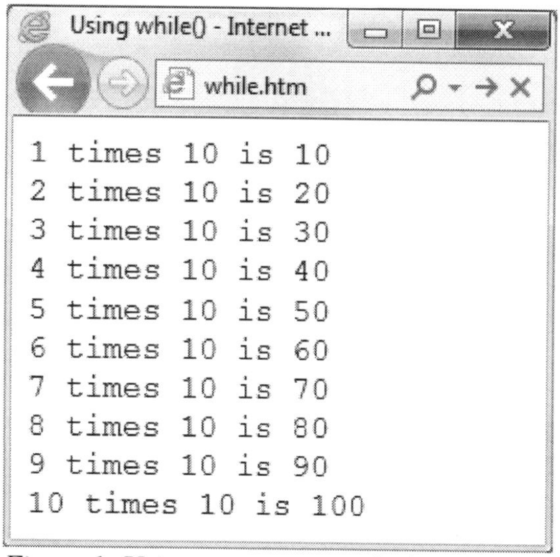

Figure 1: Using `while()` to calculate the 10 times table.

```
j = 0

while (j++ < 10)
{
   document.write(j + ' times 10 is ' + j * 10)
}
```

The code used for this and the other examples in this lecture is available in the files *while.htm*, *do_while.htm. for.htm*, *for_in.htm*, *break.htm*, and *continue.htm* in the companion archive.

The Example in Detail

This code starts by initializing the variable j to 0. This variable is used both to decide when to loop (and when to stop looping) and also for calculating the times table. Then the `while()` statement tests for j having a value of less than 10. The first time around its value is 0 so the expression evaluates to `true`. Note also that j is post-incremented after making the test by using the ++ increment operator. This means that the second time around the loop j will have a value of 1:

```
while (j++ < 10)
```

Inside the braces there is a single statement, which prints the value in j, some text and then the result of multiplying j by 10. Since j was post-incremented after the test at the start of the loop, it now has a value of 1, so the sentence '1 times 10 is 10' is output to the browser:

```
document.write(j + ' times 10 is ' + j * 10)
```

After the document.write() statement is executed the end of the loop is reached and so program flow returns to the start of the loop once more, where j is once again tested for having a value less than 10.

This time around it now has a value of 1, so that satisfies the test, and then j is post-incremented, giving it a value of 2. Therefore, this time around the loop, j has a value of 2 and so the sentence '2 times 10 is 20' is output to the browser, and the loop goes round another time.

This process continues until j has a value of 10, and the test at the start of the loop therefore no-longer results in true, so program execution jumps to just after the closing brace of the while() statement.

Note: Since there is only a single statement inside this loop, just as with for() statements, you can omit the curly braces if you wish, like this:

```
while (j++ < 10)
    document.write(j + ' times 10 is ' + j * 10)
```

Using do ... while() Loops

With a while() loop, if the test at the start is not satisfied, program execution will not flow into the loop. Sometimes, however, you want program flow to go around a loop at least once, in which case it's necessary to perform the loop test afterward.

For example, suppose you wish to calculate the factorial of the number 10 (sometimes displayed mathematically as 10!). This involves multiplying all the numbers from 1 to 10 together, like this: $10 \times 9 \times 8 \times 7 \times 6 \times 5 \times 4 \times 3 \times 2 \times 1$.

Using a loop to do this is an efficient method of calculating this value, particularly since once the loop has been built, it can be used to calculate the factorial of any number. And one thing we know for sure about this loop is that it will execute at least once. Therefore a do ... while() structure may be best suited, and you can achieve that like this:

```
j = 10
f = 1

do
{
   f *= j--
} while (j > 0)

document.write('10! is ' + f)
```

One of the neat things about this loop is that f always contains the running total of all previous multiplications, so all that's necessary to do in each iteration is multiply f by the current value in j, save that value back into f and then decrement j, which is performed by this statement:

```
f *= j--
```

As you will see, the *= assignment operator is ideal in this situation, because it performs both the multiplication and the assignment of the result back to f using a single operator. Also the post-decrement operator applied to j makes for more efficient coding too.

The Example in Detail

In detail what occurs in the preceding example is that j is a loop counter which is initialized to the value 10 (because there are ten numbers to multiply) and f is the factorial, which is initialized to 1, since the loop will start with the expression f *= j--, which the first time around the loop will be the equivalent of f = 1 * 10.

The post-decrement operator after the j ensures that each time around the loop the multiplier is decremented by one (but only after the value in j is used in the expression). So, the second time around the loop, f will now have a value of 10, and j will be 9, so the expression will be equivalent to f = 10 * 9.

Then on the next iteration, f will have a value of 90 as it enters the loop, and j will be 8, so the these two values will be multiplied together and placed back into f. The expressions evaluated in the loop are therefore as follows:

Figure 2: Using `do ... while()` *to calculate the factorial of a number.*

```
f =          1 * 10 // Results in 10
f =         10 *  9 // Results in 90
f =         90 *  8 // Results in 720
f =        720 *  7 // Results in 5040
f =       5040 *  6 // Results in 30240
f =      30240 *  5 // Results in 151200
f =     151200 *  4 // Results in 604800
f =     604800 *  3 // Results in 1314400
f =    1814400 *  2 // Results in 3628800
f =    3628800 *  1 // Results in 3628800
```

When the expression at the end of the loop (in the `while()` part) evaluates to `false`, this means that `j` is no-longer greater than 0, and so the loop is not re-entered, and program flow continues at the first instruction following the loop.

When this example is loaded into a browser (as shown in Figure 9-2), the result shown in the final line is displayed, by the `document.write()` instruction that follows the loop.

Note: As with many other JavaScript constructs, if there is only one statement inside the loop, you can omit the curly braces if you like, and the loop could therefore be written like this:

```
do f *= j--
while (j > 0)
```

Using `for()` Loops

Although the preceding to types of loop structure may seem sufficient for most requirements, they can actually be improved on, especially since you must first initialize variables outside of these loops before they are even entered, and then you generally have to increment or decrement at least one variable inside the loop, too.

For these reasons a third type of loop structure is supported, the `for()` loop, and it is one of the most compact and most-used forms of loop structure for these reasons:

- It allows you to initialize all the variables you need, within the creation of the loop.
- It allows you specify the test condition within the creation of the loop.
- It allows you to specify variables to change after each loop iteration within the creation of the loop.

Let's look at how you can do this by rewriting the previous example, as follows:

```
for (j = 10, f = 1 ; j > 0 ; --j)
{
  f *= j
}

document.write('10! is ' + f);
```

Doesn't that look much simpler than the `do ... while()` version? As before there's still a single statement inside the loop, but it no-longer uses the post-decrement operator, because `j` is decremented within the set-up section of the loop. Also there are no variables pre-assigned outside of the loop, because that is also handled within the loop set-up.

The Example in Detail

Here's what's going on. A `for()` loop's set-up section (the part within brackets) is divided into three parts which are separated with semicolons. Each part performs the following, in order:

1. Initializes any variables used within the loop.
2. Performs a test to see whether the loop should be entered.
3. Changes any variables required after each loop iteration.

The first and third sections may include more than one statement as long as you separate them using commas. Therefore in the first section of the preceding example, `j` is initialized to a value of 10, and `f` to a value of 1, like this:

```
j = 10, f = 1
```

Next comes the loop test:

```
j > 0
```

And finally j is post-decremented:

```
--j
```

With the three sets of arguments inside the brackets looking like this:

```
j = 10, f = 1 ; j > 0 ; --j
```

And that's really all there is too it. When the loop is first entered the variables are initialized. This will not happen in any other iterations. Then the test in part two of the loop set-up is made, and if the expression evaluates to true, the loop is entered.

Next the expressions in the loop are executed (in this case there's only one), and then the third section of the loop set-up is executed, which in this case decrements z.

Then, the second time and all subsequent times around the loop, section one of the set-up section is skipped and program flow goes straight to the test in section two.

If this is true then the loop is again entered, the statements in it executed, and then the statements in the third part of the set-up section are executed and the loop goes around again.

But if the test doesn't evaluate to true then program flow goes to the code following the loop, which in this case is the document.write() statement, to print the calculated factorial value.

Note: Since there is only a single statement within the loop of the preceding example the braces may legally be omitted from the code, like this (or you can make the code even more compact by placing the statement directly after the loop section):

```
for (j = 10, f = 1; j > 0 ; --j)
    f *= j
```

Generally for() loops are so powerful that they have become widespread and you will very rarely find that you need to use a while() or do ... while() loop, because for() loops can compactly and neatly accomplish almost every type of looping structure you could want in JavaScript.

Using for(... in ...) Loops

There is another type of for() loop, which is covered in much more detail in Lecture 7. Using the for(... in ...) loop you can iterate through an array of existing values in an array named Balls[] (for example), like this:

```
Balls = ['Cricket',
         'Tennis',
         'Baseball',
         'Hockey',
         'Football']

for (j in Balls)
  document.write(Balls[j] + '<br />')
```

Here the array Balls[] is populated with five string values, and then the for(... in ...) loop iterates through them all assigning an array element (from 0 through to that of the final element of the array) to the variable j, which is then used within the loop section to print out the value of each element using a document.write() statement.

The result of running this code will be as follows:

```
Cricket
Tennis
Baseball
Hockey
Football
```

Breaking Out Of a Loop

Amazingly I still haven't yet finished introducing you to everything that JavaScript loops can do for you, because there's still the matter of a couple of keywords you can employ to further enhance their use.

The first of these is the break keyword, which I already showed being used with switch() statement in Lecture 8 to stop fall-through of program flow between cases. But the break keyword is not exclusive to switch() statements. In fact it can also be used inside loops too.

But why would you want to use a break within a loop? Surely you have all the tests for conditions you could want already? Well, not quite, as it turns out. Sometimes you may

Searching for 11. Found at index 4
Searching for 17.3. Not found

Using break *to exit from a loop if a condition is met.*

As with other JavaScript structures, since this example has only a single statement in the loop, the braces can be omitted for simplicity, like this:

```
for (j = 0 ; j < Data.length ; ++j)
    if (Data[j] == 11) break
```

Note: When you use the break *keyword within a loop that is itself inside one or more other loops, only the current loop will be broken out from, because the* break *keyword applies only to the scope of the current object in which it exists.*

The continue Statement

The break statement diverts flow to the statement immediately following the loop in which it exists, but sometimes this is too drastic a measure, because you may only want to skip the current iteration of a loop, and not all remaining iterations.

When this is the case you can use the continue statement, which forces program flow to skip over any remaining statements in a loop, and to start again at the next iteration of the loop. One reason for wanting to do this might be (for example) to avoid encountering a division by zero error, which could generate invalid results.

For example, consider the case of some code that must calculate the reciprocal of all numbers between -5 and 5. The reciprocal of a number is found by dividing the value 1 by that number.

So if the number happens to be zero an attempt would be made to divide 1 by 0, which in JavaScript results in the value Infinity, which is not a floating point number that can be used in general mathematical expressions, so we need to check for it, and remove the possibility, like this:

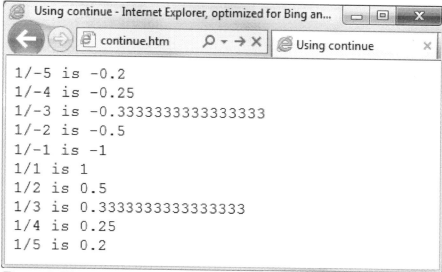

Figure 4: Using continue *to skip a loop iteration.*

```
for (j = -5 ; j < 6 ; ++j)
{
   if (j == 0) continue
   document.write('1/' + j + ' is ' + 1 / j + '<br />')
}
```

Figure 9-4 shows this code being run in a browser. As you can see, when the value 0 is reached for j, nothing is displayed, because the continue keyword has forced the loop to skip to its next iteration.

Summary

Now that you know how to use the wide variety of looping structures provided by JavaScript, you can begin to develop your own programming style, because it's now possible for you to write most types of code that rely on loops in a number of different ways, and before long you will begin to settle on the structures that fit your way of thinking the best. For example, most programmers tend to generally use for() loops, but then they may need to occasionally use the break keyword for special instances. Whereas those who prefer while() and do … while() loops rarely need to use break. It's a matter of personal style. Anyway, whichever types of loop structures you find yourself migrating towards, in the next lecture you'll discover even more powerful things you can do with JavaScript, including writing functions and using global and local variables.

JAVASCRIPT FUNCTIONS

By following this lecture you will:

- ✓ *Be able to create your own functions.*
- ✓ *Know how to pass values to and from functions.*
- ✓ *Understand the difference between local and global scope.*

As well as using conditional statements such as `if()` and `switch()`, and loops such as `while()` and `for()` there's another way you can control program flow called the *function*. Functions are sections of code that you call from any other part of code (or even the function itself, which is known as recursion), and which then perform one or more actions and then return.

When functions return they may also return a value back to the calling code, or they can simply return without doing so, in which case the returned value will be undefined. Interestingly, as you will learn in the following lecture, in JavaScript functions are also objects so they can be passed as values, used in arrays and so on.

Using Functions

JavaScript comes with many in-built functions. For example, to obtain the square root of the number 49 you can call the `Math.sqrt()` function, like this, which will return the value 7:

```
document.write(Math.sqrt(49))
```

The optional value you pass to a function is called an *argument*, and you can have any number of these arguments, or none. In the case of `Math.sqrt()` a single value is required. The square root of that number is then calculated, and the value derived is returned. That's how the `document.write()` call in the preceding example can display the square root value, because that value is returned directly to the calling code, which is the `document.write()` call.

There are two types of functions: *named* and *anonymous*. Looking for now just at named functions, you can create them using the keyword `function` followed by the name to give to the function, and then a pair of brackets, within which you list the arguments being passed to the function, separated with commas. The code of the function must be enclosed within curly braces.

Following is what the code to emulate the built-in `Math.sqrt()` function might look like, based on the fact that the square root of a number can be calculated by raising that number to the power of 0.5 – with `Math.pow()` serving to calculate the power:

```
function SquareRoot(n)
{
   return Math.pow(n, 0.5)
}
```

In this example the function created is `SquareRoot()`, and it accepts one argument (the value passed in the variable n).

The function code comprises a single statement that simply calls the in-built `Math.pow()` function, which accepts two values: a number and a value by which power the number should be raised. So the two values passed to it are n and 0.5.

The `return` Keyword

The function then calculates the square root and returns it, at which point the `return` keyword causes that value to be returned. It is then a simple matter of calling the function in the following manner to display a square root in the browser.

```
document.write(SquareRoot(49))
```

Or the value returned can be used in an expression, assigned to a variable, or used in numerous other ways.

Note: Of course, this code slightly cheats since it calls another in-built function called `Math.pow()` *(in which case we might as well simply call the in-built* `Math.sqrt()` *function in the first place), but it serves to illustrate how to write a simple function that takes one value, and returns another after processing it.*

Passing Arguments

In the preceding example you saw how to pass a single argument to a function, but you can pass as many as you need (or none), as shown with the following function that provides functionality that is not native to JavaScript (but is in some other languages), namely the ability to create a string by repeating a supplied string a set number of times.

For example, the PHP language provides a function called `str_repeat()`, and the following code gives this same functionality to JavaScript:

```
function StrRepeat(s, r)
{
   return new Array(++r).join(s)
}
```

This function uses the sneaky trick of creating a new array with the number of elements in the value r, plus 1. So if r has the value 3, then the new array is given four elements by pre-incrementing the value in r, resulting in a statement equivalent to `new Array(4)`, as described in Lecture 5.

With the array now created, the `join()` function is called by attaching it to the `Array()` function using a period. As you will recall from Lecture 7, `join()` concatenates all the elements in an array into a string, placing the separator string in the value passed to `join()` between each element value.

So if r has the value 3, a four element array is created (with each element being empty). Then the `join()` function concatenates these four elements together, placing the string in the variable s between each occurrence. Therefore, since the array elements are empty, this entire statement will simply create three copies of the string in s concatenated together, and that is the string that is returned from the function using the `return` keyword. Neat huh?

Accessing Arguments

Arguments received by a function are given the names you supply between the brackets. These do not need to be (and probably will mostly not be) the same as the variables or values passed to the function.

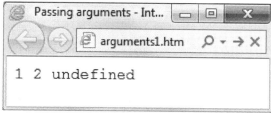

Figure 1: The third argument has not been passed to the function.

Variables are assigned to the values received by a function in the order in which they are listed, and there can be as many or as few arguments as you like. Generally the number of arguments supplied to a function should be the same as the number the function expects to receive, but not always.

If a function receives fewer arguments than it is expecting it will assign the value `undefined` to the remaining values, as shown in the following example (see Figure 10-1) in which the third argument has not been passed:

```
Example(1, 2)

function Example(a, b, c)
{
   document.write(a +' ' + b + ' ' + c)
}
```

If your function sometimes uses the missing values and sometimes doesn't, this can cause an obscure and hard to track down bug. But there are times when you may not want to provide all the arguments to a function, because they may be optional.

For example, consider the in-built JavaScript function `join()` which joins the elements of an array together into a string. It accepts either no argument, or an argument that will be used as the divider between each array element. If no argument is supplied then `join()` assumes a separator string of `', '`.

You can write code to perform the same function as `join()` like this, which creates a function of the same name, but with the first letter of the name capitalized (for simplicity I have omitted the actual code that does the joining):

```
function Join(separator)
{
   if (separator == undefined) separator = ','
   // do the joining and return the string created
}
```

The key code that provides a default value works like this:

```
if (separator == undefined) separator = ','
```

This can also be achieved using the ternary operator (as described in Lecture 4), so avoiding the use of an `if()` statement, like this:

```
separator = !separator ? ',' : separator
```

In this case the use of the `!` symbol before the `separator` variable stands in for a test for `separator` having a value of `undefined`, because it returns `true` if `separator` is undefined, and `false` if it is defined.

You can also rework this expression to not require the `!` symbol and still achieve the same result, like this (which reverses the order of the second and third arguments):

```
separator = separator ? separator : ','
```

Using The `arguments` Object

Rather than passing and accepting a known number of arguments, you can also access an object that is passed to every function called `arguments`, which contains every argument passed to the function.

You can access the elements of `arguments` as if it were an array using an index (from 0 to the number of elements in the object minus 1), or iterate through it like this:

```
for (i in arguments)
   document.write(arguments[i])
```

Note: Because the `arguments` object is not an array, even though you can find its length with `arguments.length` and can access individual elements using an index, you cannot employ any array functions on it such as `join()`, because they are set to work only with objects that are of the type `Array`.

Let's look at one example where you might find accessing this object useful, by creating a function that accepts any number of arguments and then joins them together into a string, which is returned:

```
function Deobfuscate()
{
   return arguments.join('')
}
```

This is a particularly useful function to have on hand when you wish (for example) to display an email address in a browser, but make it extremely difficult for email harvesting programs to discover, by breaking the email address (or any other section of text) that you wish to obfuscate, like this:

```
document.write(
    Deobfuscate('jame', 'sjone', 's@jjinc', '.com'))
```

This code will make little sense to even the most sophisticated email address harvester, as there are none that I know of that will actually interpret JavaScript to look for email addresses. The result of executing this statement displays in a browser as follows:

jamesjones@jjinc.com

Using The `this` Keyword

I didn't show you all the code to replicate the `join()` function in the previous section, so let's do that now, using the `this` keyword. Because `join()` can operate on an array without you passing it any argument at all, you may wonder how it knows which array it must work on. The answer is that the array is passed to `join()` using the period operator, like this:

```
Array.join()
```

When the code for the `join()` function begins execution it obtains the array in the `this` keyword, so we can finish off the new `Join()` function as follows:

```
Array.prototype.Join = Join

function Join(separator)
{
   string    = ''
   separator = !separator ? ',' : separator
```

```
    for (j = 0 ; j < this.length -1 ; ++j)
        string += this[j] + separator

    return string + this[j]
}
```

Before the function definition there is a statement that adds the ability to use the new `Join()` function on `Array` objects. It uses the `prototype` keyword, which is explained in much more detail in the following lecture. For now all you need to know is that the statement allows the function to work.

Inside the function a variable called `string` is initialized to the empty string (`''`). Its value will later be used to return the string created by this function. After that, if `separator` is not defined then it is given the default value of `','`:

```
    string = '' separator = !separator ? ',' : separator
```

Then a `for()` loop is used to iterate through all elements in the array `this`, except for the last one. You will recall that the `this` keyword contains the argument supplied via the period operator – in this case an `Array` object:

```
    for (j = 0 ; j < this.length -1 ; ++j)
```

Each time around the loop the value in the current array element is appended to the variable `string`, followed by the separator:

```
    string += this[j] + separator
```

Finally, once the loop has completed, there is one element remaining in the array that hasn't yet been accessed, and so that is appended to the end of `string`, and then the value in `string` is returned:

```
    return string + this[j]
```

Code such as the following can now be used to access the new function:

```
    Pets = ['cats', 'dogs', 'rabbits']
    document.write(Pets.Join(' and '))
```

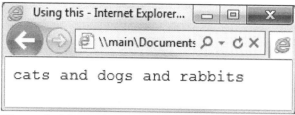

Figure 2: Using the `this` *keyword.*

This code creates a three-element array with the names of three types of pets, then it passes that array to the `Join()` function using the period operator, and also supplies the string `' and '` to be used as a separator. Figure 10-2 shows the result of loading the code (*this.htm* in the companion archive) into a browser.

Note: As well as using this to pass values using the period operator, in Lecture 13 you'll learn how the `this` *keyword is also very useful for attaching functions to JavaScript events.*

Anonymous Functions

In JavaScript it is not always necessary to give a name to a function and functions without names are called *anonymous* functions. One reason for using an anonymous function is when it is called only the once by one statement, and so for reasons of logic and code readability, the function is inserted anonymously in the code at the point where it is needed.

For example, as you will learn in Lecture 13, it is easy to attach JavaScript functions to events that occur in the browser. For example, you may want to execute a couple of actions when a mouse passes over an object, and a function is a good way to do this, as follows:

```
MyObject.onmouseover = DoThese

function DoThese()
{
  // Do this
  // DO that
  // Do the other
}
```

But if this function is only to be called at this particular point of the code you can simplify things right down by making the function anonymous, like this:

```
MyObject.onmouseover = function()
{
  // Do this
  // DO that
  // Do the other
}
```

Now you are no-longer cluttering up the JavaScript name space with the function name DoThese, and the code is shorter and sweeter.

Note: If you will want to re-use the code for a function in other places it then becomes wasteful to employ it in anonymous functions, because you will end up with several occurrences of the function's code. Therefore anonymous functions are optimal only when they will be called by a single statement.

Global and Local Variable Scope

Up to this point I have left out a very important keyword which you will certainly have seen if you have viewed the source of any JavaScript code, and that's the `var` keyword. After introducing it here, you'll see me using it a lot more. However, I left out its inclusion until now because I didn't want to get you bogged down by the difference between *local* and *global* variables. But you are ready for it now!

So far I have treated all the variables created in the course as having global scope. This means that once defined you can access their values and modify them from any other part of a program. But often this isn't completely desirable because you can start to run out of good variable names and, as a program gets longer, so will your variable names.

More than that, the larger and more complicated a program gets, and the more people working on it, the greater the chance that you may inadvertently re-assign a value to a variable that is being used in another part of the program, resulting in name clashes and weird values creeping in, creating very difficult to trace bugs.

Using Local Variables

The solution to a sprawling name space packed with numerous variable names is to allow functions to re-use a variable name, without it affecting the value of any variable with the same name used outside of the function. And the way this is achieved is with the `var` keyword.

To tell JavaScript that a variable you are using within a function should have local scope only, you simply precede it with the `var` keyword where it is first assigned a value, like this:

```
var MyVar = 42
```

From then this variable will have its value only within the function call (and any sub-functions that might be created within it). When the function returns, the variable's value is forgotten, and if there is a global variable of the same name it will resume its previous value.

Note: There is no point whatsoever in using the `var` keyword outside of a function, as you often see in examples of code on the Internet, because the program scope at that point is global and so applying local scope in a global environment results only in the variable having global scope. One reason instructors may do this, though, is when they think you may take their sample code and place it within a function. In which case it really is a good idea to make all variables that are used purely within the function have only local scope.

To illustrate how to use the `var` keyword, let's revisit the `Join()` function we looked at a little earlier, but this time with `var` keywords in the right places (shown in bold text):

```
function Join(separator)
{
  var string = ''
  separator  = !separator ? ',' : separator

  for (var j = 0 ; j < this.length -1 ; ++j)
    string += this[j] + separator

  return string + this[j]
}
```

As you'll recall this is the replacement function written to emulate the built-in `join()` function. But as previously written it was wasteful on global name space by treating both string and j as global variables, when there was no valid reason for this, and it could cause a bug if there were any existing global variables of these names.

Instead, since string and j are meant for use only in passing, the first time each is accessed (even if its inside the set-up part of a for() loop, as in this case), it is preceded by a var keyword, which ensures it will only have scope within this function.

Note: Once the var keyword has been applied to a variable it does not need to be done again. The local scope will remain until the function returns.

In the following example the variable Fred is assigned the value 1. Because the assignment occurs outside of any functions it has global scope, which means its value can be accessed from any part of the program.

However, within the function MyFunc() the variable Fred is re-used, but with the var keyword preceding it, so it has local scope only.

```
Fred = 1
document.write('Fred is ' + Fred + '<br />')
MyFunc()
document.write('Fred is ' + Fred + '<br />')

function MyFunc()
{
  var Fred = 2
  document.write('Fred is ' + Fred + '<br />')
}
```

Following the program flow, at the first document.write() call Fred has a value of 1. Then MyFunc() is called and, within the function, the local variable Fred is assigned the value 2. After displaying its value the function returns (no return keyword is used since there is no value to return from this function).

Upon return the value in Fred is again displayed, and it is back to 1 again, because when Fred is referred to outside of the function, it refers to the global variable, whose value remains unchanged at 1

Figure 10-3 (created with *var.htm* in the companion archive) shows the result of running this code in a browser.

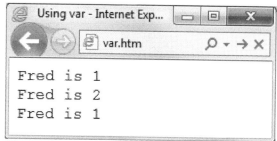

Figure 3: Using local and global variables of the same name.

Note: *What is happening here is that two separate variables have been used. They may have the same name, but because the one in the function is given local scope, it is quite different to the one outside the function. I would also like to mention in passing that the keyword* var *is not actually very helpful in that it doesn't really describe what it does. In my view the keyword* local *would have been a much better choice. Nevertheless,* var *is the word that has been chosen – just remember that it always applies local scope (and only works within a function).*

Global Naming Convention

I write a lot of JavaScript code and found that for each variable used I would still have to keep referring back to see whether it had a var keyword applied at any point in a function (making it local), or if no var keyword was used it would then be global. To save me from having to keep rechecking I came up with the following simple convention.

Whenever a variable is created that should have global scope I use all uppercase letters, like this:

```
HIGHSCORE  = 0   // Creates a global variable
HighScore += 100 // Increments a local variable
```

Therefore any variables I use that have any lowercase letters I can be sure are being used as local variables, and I also ensure I use the var keyword on their first use in a function.

Of course, you can use any other convention you like (such as prefacing global variables with G_), or no convention at all.

Note: You might ask whether separating global and local variables by uppercase and lowercase obviates the need for the `var` keyword, since local variables will never compete with global ones. However that's not the case because all variables would then be global and we would be back at having to choose lots of different non-uppercase variable names for use in functions to avoid them conflicting with each other. So, using uppercase for global variables simply makes it clear at a glance which ones are and aren't global, so you never have to go hunting for `var` keywords to understand the various scopes of variables in a complex function.

Summary

Congratulations. With the use of functions under your belt you can now call yourself a JavaScript programmer. However, there are still a few more steps to take before you can call yourself a master of the language – starting in the following lecture with JavaScript objects, which enable you to write OOP (Object Oriented Programming).

JavaScript Objects

By following this lecture you will:

✓ *Understand how everything in JavaScript is an object.*

✓ *Know how to create object classes.*

✓ *Be able to create and use objects.*

JAVASCRIPT IS AN interesting language in that everything in it is an object. Arrays are objects, functions are objects, variables are objects, and so on, although they are objects of different types, or should I say *class*.

You see, by being structured this way, JavaScript is extremely easy to enhance, by adding new classes (or types) of object, and then creating objects using these classes with the `new` keyword, as you've seen used for creating new arrays, for example.

You've also seen the `prototype` keyword used to allow a new function to be created to extend the JavaScript language by (for example), adding new functions to manipulate objects of the type `Array`. In this chapter I'll bring all these things (and more) together and show how you can create truly object oriented programs (OOP).

Declaring a Class

The first step in object oriented programming is declaring a class, which defines a new type of object, but doesn't actually create the object. Classes group together a combination of data and the program code required to manipulate the data, into a single object.

To declare a class you use the same syntax as for a function (since functions in JavaScript are actually objects), like this:

```
function UserClass(firstname, lastname)
{
  this.firstname = firstname
  this.lastname  = lastname

  this.getName = function()
  {
    return this.firstname + ' ' + this.lastname
  }
}
```

This code is known as a class *constructor*. It creates the new class `UserClass` and gives it two items of data it can hold: `firstname`, and `lastname`.

It also sets up a method (another name for a function) that can be applied to the class called `getName()`, which returns a string with `firstname` and `lastname` concatenated together, separated with a space character.

Note: See how the `this` keyword is used here to reference objects created using this class, and also the functions supplied to access the data in the object. You will also have noticed how an anonymous function is assigned to `this.getName`. This is good use of an anonymous function as it's the only place the function is accessed. However a name does get indirectly assigned to this function after all, because the function can be accessed through calling the `getName()` method on any objects created from the class.

Creating an Object

You can now create a new object (known as an *instance*) based on this class, as follows (in which the new object `User` is created):

```
User = new UserClass()
```

This creates the new object `User`, which has all the properties and methods defined in the class. The object doesn't (yet) have any data in it, though.

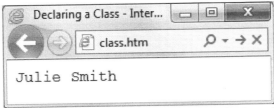

Figure 1: Calling the `getName()` *method on the* `User` *object.*

By the way. In JavaScript the terms *method* and *function* mean the same thing and are interchangeable. However, I choose to refer to a function by the name method only when it is provided as part of a class declaration, and is therefore a method that can be used on objects that are instances of the class. And I reserve the term function for stand-alone functions that are not part of object oriented programming.

Accessing Objects

Once an instance of a class has been created using the `new` keyword, you can populate the object with data like this:

```
User.firstname = 'Julie'
User.lastname  = 'Smith'
```

Or, alternatively, you can pre-populate the object (in the same manner as pre-populating a new array) when you create the instance of the class, like this:

```
User = new UserClass('Julie', 'Smith')
```

Thereafter you can read these properties back by accessing them in the following manner:

```
document.write(User.firstname)
```

And you can update object properties (in the case of this instance, for example) with a change of the user's last name, like this:

```
User.lastname = 'Jones'
```

And you can call any of the methods provided by an object's class, such as the `getName()` method of the `UserClass` class, like this:

```
document.write(User.getName())
```

Figure 11-1 shows the result of running the preceding code (available as *class.htm* in the companion archive) in a browser.

The `prototype` Keyword

The `prototype` keyword can save you a lot of memory. For example, in the `UserClass` class, every instance will contain the two properties and the method. Therefore, if you have a thousand of these objects in memory, the method `getName()` will also be replicated a thousand times – this is highly wasteful.

However, because the method is identical in every case, you can specify that new objects should refer to a single instance of the method only, instead of creating a copy of it. To do this, instead of using the following in a class constructor:

```
this.getName = function()
```

You can replace the statement with this:

```
UserClass.prototype.getName = function()
```

What is happening here is that instead of attaching the function to the `this` keyword (which would cause multiple instances of the function), the function is attached directly to the class `UserClass` via the `prototype` keyword.

All methods have a `prototype` property which is designed to hold properties and methods that are not to be replicated in objects created from the class. Instead, when the `prototype` keyword is used the method (or property) is passed by *reference*, so that there will only be one instance of the method (or property).

This passing by reference means you can add a prototype property or method to a class at any time and all objects (even those already created) will inherit it. For example, If you wish to create a standard message that will be used to create users logging into a website, you could extend the `UserClass` class with the following:

```
UserClass.prototype.Greeting = 'Welcome back '
```

This type of method or property (created using the `prototype` keyword) is known as *static*. A static method or property has a single instance which is accessible from any object created from a class.

You can display this single instance of the property at any time from any object created from the class, like this:

```
document.write(User.Greeting)
```

You could then expand the getName() method to supply the greeting, like this:

```
UserClass.prototype.getName = function()
{
   return this.Greeting + this.firstname + ' ' +
     this.lastname
}
```

Now, when getName() is called on the object, it will display the following (pulling the Greeting string from the prototype of the class, so that only a single instance of the string exists, no-matter how many instances of the object there are):

Welcome back Julie Smith

Extending JavaScript Functions

In Lecture 10 I briefly glossed over the prototype keyword when showing you how to attach a new function (now called a method, since we're discussing object oriented programming) to objects of the type Array. Now that you have read this far you should understand exactly what was going on.

In the replacement Join() method, the Array class has its prototype property updated by adding to it a new method called Join().

Below I have updated the example by assigning the method directly to the prototype keyword (rather than first creating the method, giving it a name, and then assigning that name to the prototype keyword, as was previously the case):

```
Array.prototype.Join = function(separator)
{
   var string = ''
   separator  = !separator ? ',' : separator

   for (var j = 0 ; j < this.length -1 ; ++j)
      string += this[j] + separator
```

```
    return string + this[j]
  }
```

You should now see how this code simply adds a new static method to the `Array` class, so that it can be called on any object of that type, like this:

```
MyArray.Join()
```

You can extend any of JavaScript's classes in a similar manner, even to the point of rewriting it to work the way you prefer, as is the case with frameworks such as *jQuery* (see *jquery.com*), which extensively extend JavaScript to provide a wide range of additional functionality.

For example, if you wanted to make the `StrRepeat()` function from lecture 10 operate as a method on `String` objects, you could use the following code to add a method called `Repeat()`:

```
String.prototype.Repeat = function(r)
{
   return new Array(++r).join(this)
}
```

Then, for example, to display the string `'Hip, Hip, Hooray. '` three times, you can use the following statement (as shown in Figure 11-2):

```
document.write('Hip, Hip, Hooray. '.Repeat(3))
```

Note: In the preceding example, rather than attaching to a string variable, the `repeat()` method is attached directly to a string. To JavaScript this is the same thing because such a string is an object of type `String`.

Summary

You are now becoming a power JavaScript programmer, capable of bending the will of the language itself to your desire. All that remains to finish your training (before moving onto using JavaScript in meaningful ways in your web pages) is to flesh your knowledge out a bit by looking at things such as how to gracefully handle errors in your code, and how to use regular expressions for powerful pattern matching – both of which are in the following lecture.

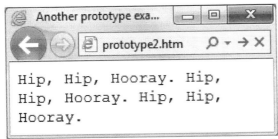

Figure 2: Implementing a new `Repeat()` *method.*

ERRORS AND EXPRESSIONS

By following this lecture you will:

- ✓ *Learn how to trap and handle errors.*
- ✓ *Use regular expressions for pattern matching.*
- ✓ *Be able to search and replace complex strings.*

THERE'S NO GETTING away from it, even the most careful programmers build unexpected errors (or bugs) into their code, and so will you – it's perfectly normal. And even after you think you've fully debugged your code the likelihood remains that there may still be obscure bugs lurking somewhere.

The last thing you want on a published website is for users to encounter errors, or sometimes even worse, just find your code doesn't work for them – making them leave to never return.

But JavaScript comes with ways you can minimize the problem by placing helper code around statements where you suspect a bug may be that will take over if one occurs.

In this lecture I'll show you how you can use JavaScript's in-built error trapping for dealing with bugs, and even for managing cross-browser compatibility. I'll also be showing you how you can use regular expressions to perform powerful and complex pattern matching in single statements.

Using `onerror`

The simplest way to catch errors in your code is to attach a new function to the `onerror` event, like this:

```
window.onerror = function(msg, url, line)
{
   var temp = url.split('/')
   url       = temp[temp.length - 1]

   alert('Error in line ' + line + ' of ' +
      url + '\n\n' + msg)
}
```

The onerror event passes three values to a function attached to it: an error message, the URL of the page where the error was encountered, and the line number of the error. The new function in the preceding example accepts these values in the variables msg, url and line.

The function code then calls the in-built JavaScript split() function, which splits a string (in this case url) at whatever character is supplied to it (in this case '/') into an array of elements containing each of the parts split out from the string, like this:

```
var temp = url.split('/')
```

Then the final element (indexed by temp.length -1) is placed back into the variable url, like this:

```
url = temp[temp.length - 1]
```

The result of these two lines of code is to strip any path details from url, leaving only the name of the file in which the error occurred. If this is not done, on deeply nested pages a very large string would be displayed, making the error message very hard to read.

Having shortened url, the in-built JavaScript alert() function is called, passing it the details to display, like this:

```
alert('Error in line ' + line + ' of ' +
   url + '\n\n' + msg)
```

So, for example, with this function in place, if you then introduce a mistake into your code such as the following example (in which the final e is omitted from document.write), the result will be similar to Figure 12-1:

```
document.writ('Test')
```

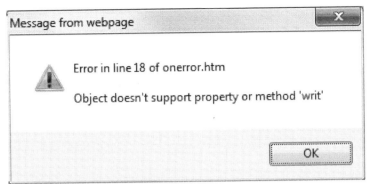

Figure 1: Attaching to the `onerror` *event.*

Note: *Rather than using* `<br />` *tags to obtain the newlines in the alert dialog (which will not work because dialog boxes don't support HTML) I have used the string* `'\n\n'`, *which sends the newlines as escape characters.*

Using this function you can quickly and easily catch the bulk of bugs in your code before transferring it to a production server. I don't recommend leaving this function in place on customer-facing websites, though.

It would probably be better to write a more obscure message along the lines of "Sorry, this web page encountered an error, please try again". Hopefully whatever caused the error will not be in place on the second attempt, as you will have thoroughly debugged most non-obscure bugs already.

Using `try ... catch()`

Rather than just catching errors and displaying debugging information, you can go a step further and choose to ignore errors that may be trivial.

For example, if you have some code that you know works only in some browsers but causes errors in others, it would be a shame to not allow the added functionality to at least some of your users. And you can do this by placing such code in a `try ... catch()` structure.

The way you do this is as follow, in which the code to try and code to call upon the first code causing an error are placed in the two parts of the structure:

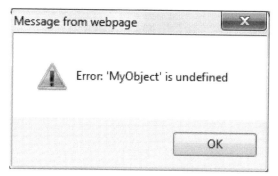

Figure 2: Using `try` *and* `catch()`.

```
try
{
  // Place code to try here.
}
catch(e)

  // Place alternate code here.
}
```

The argument passed to the `catch()` part of the structure is an error object, which can be used for obtaining the error message by displaying its `message` property, like this (as shown in Figure 12-2 in which an attempt to access the object `MyObject` has failed as it doesn't exist):

```
catch(e)
{
  alert('Error: ' + e.message)
}
```

The code used for creating Figure 12-2 is in the *try_catch.htm* file in the accompanying archive.

Ignoring the Error

If you wish you can ignore the error object and simply get on with executing alternate code. For example, you will see the following code used in Lecture 14 for creating an object with which Ajax (Asynchronous JavaScript And XML) background communication can be initiated with a web server:

```
try
{
  var ajax = new XMLHttpRequest()
}
catch(e1)
{
  try
  {
    ajax = new ActiveXObject("Msxml2.XMLHTTP")
  }
  catch(e2)
  {
    try
    {
      ajax = new ActiveXObject("Microsoft.XMLHTTP")
    }
    catch(e3)
    {
      ajax = false
    }
  }
}
```

For reasons that are explained in Lecture 14 it can take up to three attempts to create an Ajax object, depending on the browser used, and the preceding code handles all this gracefully to return an Ajax object in `ajax` – if the browser supports it.

Regular Expressions

Regular expressions were invented as a means of matching an enormous variety of different types of pattern with just a single expression. Using them you can replace several lines of code with a simple expression, and can even use regular expressions in replace as well as search operations.

To properly learn everything there is to know about regular expressions could take a whole book (and, indeed, books have been written on the subject), so I'm just going to introduce you to the basics in this lecture, but if you need to know more I recommend you check out the following URL as a good starting point:

wikipedia.org/wiki/Regular_expression

In JavaScript you will use regular expressions mostly in two functions: `test()` and `replace()`. The `test()` function tells you whether its argument matches the regular expression, while `replace()` takes a second parameter: the string to replace the text that matches.

Using `test()`

Let's say you want to find out whether one string occurs within another. For example, if you wish to know if the string `'whether'` occurs in Hamlet's famous soliloquy you might use code such as the following:

```
s = "To be, or not to be, that is the question: "    +
    "Whether 'tis Nobler in the mind to suffer"      +
    "The Slings and Arrows of outrageous Fortune, " +
    "Or to take Arms against a Sea of troubles, "    +
    "And by opposing end them."

RegExp = /whether/
document.write(RegExp.test(s))
```

Note: The `test()` function requires passing of the regular expression to it via the period operator, and the string to be searched must be passed as an argument between the brackets.

In this example the object `RegExp` is a regular expression object that is given the value `/whether/`, which is how you denote a regular expression. First you place a / character, then the text to match, followed by a closing / character.

In this example, however, a match is not made because (by default) regular expressions are case-sensitive, and only the word `Whether` (with an upper case `W`) exists in the string.

If you wish to make a case-insensitive search you can tell JavaScript by placing the letter `i` after the closing / character, like this (in this case a match will be made):

```
RegExp = /whether/i
```

You don't have to place a regular expression in an object first if you choose not to, so the two lines can be replaced with the following single statement:

```
document.write(/whether/i.test(s))
```

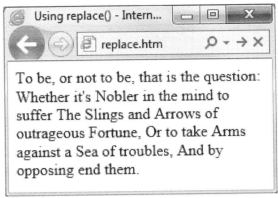

Figure 3: Applying `replace()` *to a string.*

Using `replace()`

You can also replace text that matches using the `replace()` function. The source string is not modified by this because `replace()` returns a new string with all the changes made.

So, for example, to replace the string `'tis` in the soliloquy with the word `it's` (although Shakespeare would surely object), you could use a regular expression and the `replace()` function like this:

```
document.write(s.replace(/'tis/, "it's"))
```

Note: *The* `replace()` *function takes its arguments differently to* `test()`. *Firstly it requires that the string for matching against is passed to it via the period operator. Then it takes two arguments in brackets: the regular expression, and the string to replace it with.*

Figure 12-3 shows the result of executing this statement (using the file *replace.htm* in the accompanying archive). In it you can see that the word after `Whether` is now `it's`.

As with `test()` you can specify a case-insensitive replace by placing an `i` character at the end of the regular expression, as in the following example, which replaces the first occurrence of the word `to` in any combination of upper and lower case, with the word `TO` in upper case:

```
document.write(s.replace(/to/i, "TO"))
```

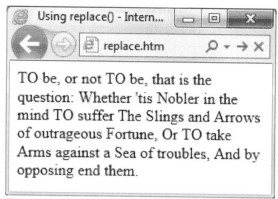

Figure 4: Performing a global, case-insensitive replace operation.

Replacing Globally

You can also choose to conduct a global replacement and replace all occurrences of a match by placing the character g after the expression, as follows:

```
document.write(s.replace(/to/ig, "TO"))
```

In the preceding example both the characters i and g have been placed after the expression, so this causes a global, case-insensitive search and replace operation, resulting in Figure 12-4 in which you can see all incidences of the word to have been changed to upper case.

Fuzzy Matching

Regular expressions are a lot more powerful than simply searching for and replacing words and phrases, because they also support complex fuzzy logic features through the use of *metacharacters*.

There are several types of metacharacter but let's look at just one for now, the * character, to see how they work. When you place a * in a regular expression it is not treated as that asterisk character, but as a metacharacter with a special meaning, which is that when performing a match the character immediately preceding the * may appear in the searched string any number of times (or not at all).

This type of metacharacter is particularly useful for sweeping up lots of blank space so that you can, for example, search for any of the strings 'back pack', 'backpack', `'back pack'` (with two spaces between the words), `'Back Pack'` (with mixed case), and many other combinations, like this:

```
s = "Have you seen my BackPack anywhere?"

document.write(/back *pack/i.test(s))
```

Because the `i` character is also used the matching is case-insensitive, and so the word `BackPack` is found by the regular expression, and the `document.write()` call displays the result of `true` in the browser.

Note: If you want to use any of the characters that are metacharacters as regular characters in your regular expressions you must escape them by preceding the characters with a \ character. For example * will turn the * from a metacharacter into a simple asterisk.

Matching Any Character

You can get even fuzzier than that, though, with the period (or dot) character, which can stand in for any character at all (except a newline). For example to find all HTML tags (which start with < and end with >) you could use the following regular expression (in either a `test()` or `replace()` call):

```
/<.*>/
```

The left and right angle brackets either side serve as the start and end points for each match. Within them this expression will match any character due to the dot metacharacter, while the * after the dot says there can be zero, one or any number of these characters. Therefore any size of HTML tag, from the meaningless <> upwards will be matched.

Other metacharacters include the + symbol, which works like the *, except that it will match one or more characters, so you could avoid matching <> by ensuring there is always at least one character between the angle brackets, like this:

```
/<.+>/
```

Unfortunately, because the * and + characters will match all the way up to the last > on a line, as well as catching single tags like `<h1>Heading</h1>`, they can also catch nested HTML such as `<h1><i>Heading</i></h1>`.

Metacharacters	Action
/	Begins and ends a regular expression
.	Matches any character other than newline
*	Matches previous element zero or more times
+	Matches previous element one or more times
?	Matches previous element zero or one time
[*characters*]	Matches a single character out of those contained within the brackets
[^*characters*]	Matches a single character that is not contained within the brackets
(*regexp*)	Treats *regexp* as a group for counting, or following *, + or ?
left|*right*	Matches either *left* or *right*
l-r	(Within square brackets) Matches a range of characters between *l* and *r*
^	(Outside of square brackets) Requires the match to be at the search string's start
$	(Outside of square brackets) Requires the match to be at the search string's end

Table 12-1: The basic metacharacters.

Not Matching a Character

A solution to the multi-tag matching problem is to use the ^ character whose meaning is 'anything but', but which must be placed within square brackets, like this:

```
[^>]+
```

This regular expression is like .+ except there is one character it refuses to match, the > symbol. Therefore, when presented with the string `<h1><i>Heading</i></h1>`, the expression will now stop at the first > encountered, and so the initial `<h1>` tag will be properly matched.

Other	Action
\b	Matches a word boundary
\B	Matches where there isn't a word boundary
\d	Matches a digit
\D	Matches a non-digit
\n	Matches a newline character
\s	Matches a whitespace character
\S	Matches a non-whitespace character
\t	Matches a tab character
\w	Matches one of a-z, A-Z, 0-9 or _
\W	Matches any character but a-z, A-Z, 0-9 or _
\x	(Where x is a metacharacter) Treats x as a normal character
{n}	Matches exactly n times
{$n,$}	Matches n times or more
{min,max}	Matches at least min and at most max times

Table 12-2: Escape and numeric range metacharacters.

Table 12-1 summarizes the basic metacharacters and their actions.

Some of the characters in Table 12-1 I have already explained, while some should be self-explanatory. Others, however you may find confusing, so I would recommend only using those you understand until you have learned more about regular expressions, perhaps from the Wikipedia article listed a little earlier.

There is also a selection of escape metacharacters and numeric ranges you can include, listed in Table 12-2. To help you better understand how these various metacharacters can work together, in Table 12-3 I have detailed a selection of regular expression examples, and the matches they will make.

Example	Matches
`\.`	The first . in *Hello there. Nice to see you.*
`h`	The first h *in My hovercraft is full of eels*
`lemon`	The word *lemon* in *I like oranges and lemons*
`orange|lemon`	Either *orange* or *lemon* in I like oranges and lemons
`bel[ei][ei]ve`	Either *believe* or *beleive* (also *beleeve* or *beliive*)
`bel[ei]{2}ve`	Either *believe* or *beleive* (also *beleeve* or *beliive*)
`bel(ei)|(ie)ve`	Either *believe* or *beleive* (but not *beleeve* or *beliive*)
`2\.0*`	*2., 2.0, 2.00* and so on
`j-m`	Any of the characters *j, k, l,* or *m*
`house$`	Only the final *house* in *This house is my house*
`^can`	Only the first *can* in *can you open this can?*
`\d{1,2}`	And one or two digit number from *0* to *9* and *00* to *99*
`[\w]+`	Any word of at least one character
`[\w]{3}`	Any three letter word

Table 12-3: Some example regular expressions and their matches.

Remember that you can place the character `i` after the closing / of a regular expression to make it case-insensitive, and place a `g` to perform a global search (or replace).

You can also place the character `m` after the final / which puts the expression into multi-line mode, so that the ^ and $ characters will match at the start and end of any newlines in the string, rather than the default of the string's start and end.

Note: *You may use any combination of the* `i`, `g` *and* `m` *modifiers after your regular expressions.*

Summary

This lecture has covered some fairly advanced things, including error handling and sophisticated pattern matching, and it tops off the last items of basic knowledge you need about the JavaScript language. Starting with the following lecture I will, therefore, concentrate on how to use JavaScript to interact with web pages, commencing with understanding how JavaScript integrates with the Document Object Model (DOM) of HTML to create dynamic functionality.

THE DOCUMENT OBJECT MODEL

By following this lecture you will:

- ✓ *Know how JavaScript hooks into the Document Object Model.*
- ✓ *Be able to manipulate HTML elements directly.*
- ✓ *Learn how to attach your own functions to JavaScript events.*

THE DOCUMENT OBJECT Model (DOM) separates the different parts of an HTML document into a hierarchy of objects, each one having its own *properties*. The term property is used for referring to an attribute of an object such as the HTML it contains, its width and height, and so on.

The outermost object possible is the window object, which is the current browser window, tab, iframe or popped up window. Underneath this is the document object, of which there can be more than one (such as several documents loaded into different iframes within a page). And inside a document there are other objects such as the head and body of a page.

Within the head there can be other objects such as the title and meta objects, while the body object can contain numerous other objects, including headings, anchors, forms and so forth.

For example, Figure 13-1 shows a representation of the DOM of an example document, with the document title of *Example*, a meta tag in the head, and three HTML elements (a link, a form, and an image) in the body section.

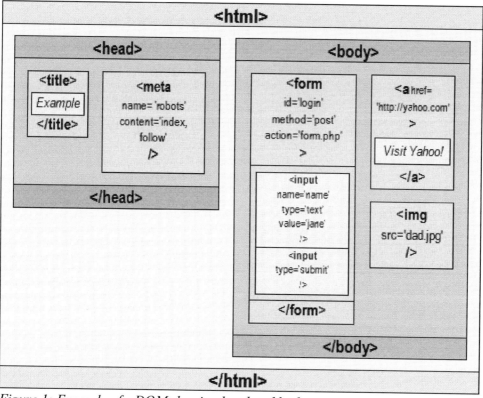

Figure 1: Example of a DOM showing head and body sections.

The source of this example web page looks like this:

```
<html>
  <head>
    <title>Example</title>
    <meta name='robots' content='index, follow' />
  </head>
  <body>
    <a href='http://yahoo.com'>Visit Yahoo!</a>
    <form id='login' method='post' action='form.php'>
      <input name='name' type='text' value='jane' />
      <input type='submit' />
    </form>
    <img src='dad.jpg' />
  </body>
</html>
```

Starting with the `<head>` section you can see that there are two elements. The first is the document's title of `'Example'`, contained within `<title>` and `</title>` tags, while the second is the meta tag that tells search engine crawlers that the document may be crawled, its contents indexed and any links can be followed:

```
<title>Example</title>
<meta name='robots' content='index, follow' />
```

This is done by passing the value `robots` to the `name` attribute, and the string `'index, follow'` to the `content` attribute. Meta tags are self-closing so there is no `</meta>` tag. The section is then closed with a `</head>` tag:

```
</head>
```

Next is the body of the document, which is contained within `<body>` and `</body>` tags. There are three elements in this section, a link to `'http://yahoo.com'` in `<a>` and `</a>` tags, an embedded image that uses a self-closing `<img />` tag, and a form contain within `<form>` and `</form>` tags:

```
<body>
  <a href='http://yahoo.com'>Visit Yahoo!</a>
  <form id='login' method='post' action='form.php'>
    <input name='name' type='text' value='jane' />
    <input type='submit' />
  </form>
  <img src='dad.jpg' />
</body>
```

The form passes a value of `'login'` to the `id` attribute, `'post'` to the `method` attribute, and the program name `'form.php'` (the program that is to process the form when it is submitted) is assigned to the `action` attribute:

```
<form id='login' method='post' action='form.php'>
```

The method used for sending the data to the server is specified by the `method` argument. Its value can be other `'post'` or `'get'`. This example uses a `'post'` request which sends the data in a hidden manner. (A `'get'` request would pass the posted data by attaching it after the URL in what is known as a query string.)

Inside the form there are two self-closing `<input />` tags. The first passes the string value `'name'` to the `name` attribute, `'text'` to the `type` attribute, and the value `'jane'` to the `value` attribute. This pre-populates the input field with the word `'jane'` but it can be altered by the user:

```
<input name='name' type='text' value='jane' />
```

After this a second `<input />` tag creates a submit button by passing the value `'submit'` to its `type` attribute:

```
<input type='submit' />
```

Finally the form is closed with a `</form>` tag, and the image is displayed:

```
</form>
<img src='dad.jpg' />
```

When opened in a browser the document looks something like Figure 13-2.

Accessing the DOM From JavaScript

Now let's look at how elements can be manipulated from JavaScript, which (as you know) should always be placed within `<script>` and `</script>` tags, which these examples assume have already been applied. For example, the following code changes the document's title to `'An example web page'`:

```
document.title = 'An example web page'
```

As you will recall, JavaScript uses the period operator to either pass the current object to a function (or method), or to reference properties of objects. In this case `title` is a property of the `document` object, so this statement has the same effect as if you opened the document in a program editor and directly edited the title within the `<title>` and `</title>` tags yourself.

Similarly the form method type of `'post'` (in the example in the previous section) could be easily changed to `'get'`, like this:

```
document.forms.login.method = 'get'
```

Here the JavaScript references first the `document`, then the `forms` within that document, then the form with the `id` of `login` and its `method`, which is then modified.

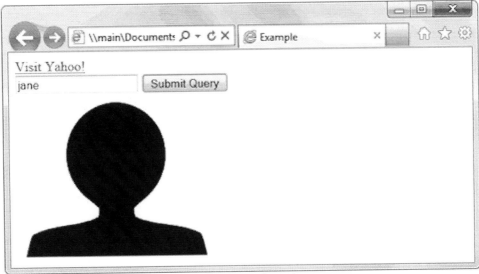

Figure 2: The result of displaying the example web page.

Using the `getElementById()` Function

In the previous couple of examples I showed you how to access parts of a document by their type, but there's a far, far easier method, which is to give every element in a document a unique id, and then to access them from JavaScript using just those ids.

For example, if the `<img />` tag is given an id (such as `'image1'`) with which it can be identified, it's possible to replace the image loaded by it with another, as with the following code, in which the male-shaped `dad.jpg` image is replaced with `mom.jpg` to match the default name in the form field of `'jane'`:

```
<img src='dad.jpg' id='image1' />

<script>
    document.getElementById('image1').src = 'mom.jpg'
</script>
```

The trick here is to use the JavaScript function `getElementById()` which will let you access any DOM element that has been given a unique id. So let's look at another example by restoring the previous name and image mismatch by altering the default `name` value directly, rather that accessing the element via `document.forms.login`.

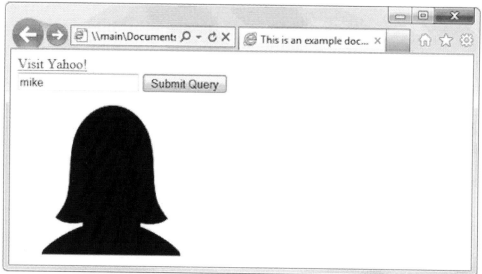

Figure 3: Three elements of the page have been modified with JavaScript

By giving the form field an id (such as 'name') and using getElementById() we can avoid the long-windedness of the previous example and go straight to the element to change it, like this (in which I have shown only the updated <input /> tag HTML, and not the remainder of the HTML – which remains unchanged):

```
<input name='name' type='text' value='jane' id='name' />

<script>
   document.getElementById('name').value = 'mike'
</script>
```

See how much easier it is than having to remember whether an element is part of a form, an image or something else? All you have to do is know the id of an element and getElementById() will do the job of finding it for you.

Figure 13-3 shows how the web page now displays after these changes. The title is different, the default input value is 'mike' and the image shown is mom.jpg (yes, the gender is all confused again).

The Simpler O() Function

I use the `getElementById()` function so often that I have created a simple function called O() (with an upper case O) to make it quicker to type in. The function looks like this and I place it at the start of any JavaScript, right after the opening `<script>` tag, like this:

```
<script>
  function O(obj)
  {
     return document.getElementById(obj)
  }
</script>
```

Doing this saves 22 characters of typing each time the replacement O() function is used instead of the longer one.

One reason for the tremendous shortening is because the preceding `document.` has also been incorporated into the O() function, saving on typing that in too, as you can see if you compare the following long and short versions:

```
document.getElementById('name').value = 'mike'
O('name').value = 'mike'
```

However, there's one further step I like to take that makes the function even more useful and that's to allow the passing to it of either element `id`s (which is what it does so far), or an object that has already been created (possibly as the result of previously having called the O() function).

Let me explain it like this. Instead of manipulating the `value` of the form input with the `id` of `'name'` directly, let's first create an object from this element, like this:

```
newobject = O('name')
```

Now that I have this object I can access as often as I like without ever having to call the O() function again, like this for example (in which the value is changed on separate occasions):

```
newobject.value = 'mike'
   // A few lines of code go here
newobject.value = 'fred'
```

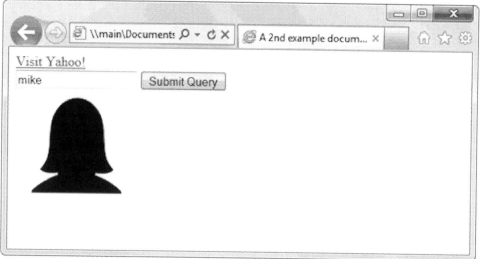

Figure 4: The mom.jpg image has been reduced in size

However, I am a lazy programmer (as are all 'good' programmers). Once I have created a function I like to re-use it rather than write a new one, and there are times when I would also like to pass either an object to the O() function (as you'll see in the following section), or an id name.

Therefore I prefer to use the following version of the function, which supports either type of argument:

```
function O(obj)
{
   if (typeof obj == 'object') return obj
   else return document.getElementById(obj)
}
```

What is happening here is that the argument passed in `obj` is analyzed by the code and if it happens to already be of the type `object` then the object is simply returned, because it is already an object. But if it is not of that type then it is assumed to be an `id` name, in which case it is looked up and returned as an object with a call to `getElementById()`.

The Partner S() Function

In a similar fashion to the space saving produced by using the O() function, there is one other function that I employ frequently because its action is also used all the time in

JavaScript, and that's the new function S() (with an upper case S). I use this to enable JavaScript to easily access any `style` attribute of any element.

For example, if I wish to change the `width` and `height` of the image I can do it like this (which results in Figure 4, when the other lines of HTML and JavaScript we've been using are included):

```
<img src='mom.jpg' id='image1' />

<script>
  O('image1').style.width = '150px' // Longer syntax
  S('image1').height      = '120px' // Shorter syntax

function O(obj)
{
  if (typeof obj == 'object') return obj
  else return document.getElementById(obj)
}

  function S(obj)
  {
    return O(obj).style
  }
</script>
```

What I've done here is simply make the S() function place a call to the O() function but with an added `.style` suffix, and now I can use O() for accessing elements by name, and S() for accessing the style attributes of elements by name.

What's more, because the O() function allows either `id` names or objects, I can pass either type of argument to S() as well. So, if I have an object called `myobject` (perhaps previously created using the O() function) I can change its `width` property like this:

```
S(myobject).width = '100px'
```

This code can be quicker as the object is only looked up once, and is therefore a more efficient way to code when an element may be accessed more than once. This works because you are allowed to enter <script> tags as many times as you like in a document – there is no requirement to keep all your JavaScript code within a single set of <script> and </script> tags, although you may do so if you wish.

Accessing Multiple Elements by Class

So far I've provided you with two simple function that make it easy for you to access any element on a web page, and any `style` property of an element. Sometimes, though, you will want to access more than one element at a time and you can do this by assigning a CSS class name to each such element, like these examples:

```
<div class='MyClass'>Div contents</a>
<p id='MyClass'>Paragraph contents</p>
```

Then you can use the following handy `C()` (short for Class) function to return an array containing all the objects that match the class name provided:

```
function C(name)
{
  var elements = document.getElementsByTagName('*')
  var objects  = []

  for (var i = 0 ; i < elements.length ; ++i)
    if (elements[i].className == name)
      objects.push(elements[i])

  return objects
}
```

Let's break this down. First the argument `name` contains the class name to reference then, inside the function, a new object called `elements` is created which contains all the elements in the document, as returned by a call to `getElementsByTagName()` with an argument of `'*'`, which means find all elements:

```
var elements = document.getElementsByTagName('*')
```

Then a new array called `objects` is created, into which all the matching objects found will be placed:

```
var objects = []
```

Next a `for()` loop iterates through all the elements in the `elements` object using the variable `i` as the index:

```
for (var i = 0 ; i < elements.length ; ++i)
```

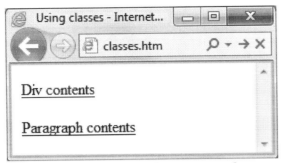

Figure 5: Modifying all elements in a class.

Each time around the loop, if an element's `className` property is the same as the string value passed in the argument `name`, then the object is pushed onto the `objects[]` array:

```
if (elements[i].className == name)
  objects.push(elements[i])
```

Finally, once the loop has completed, the `objects[]` array will contain all the elements in the document that use the class name in `name`, so it is returned by the function:

```
return objects
```

Using the C() Function

To use the function simply call it like this, saving the returned array so that you can access each of the elements individually as required or, more likely to be the case, en-masse via a loop:

```
MyArray = C('MyClass')
```

Now you can do whatever you like with the objects returned, such as (for example) setting their `textDecoration` style property to `'underline'`, as follows:

```
for (i = 0 ; i < MyArray.length ; ++i)
  S(MyArray[i]).textDecoration = 'underline'
```

This code iterates through the objects in `MyArray[]` and then uses the `S()` function to reference each one's `style` property, setting its `textDecoration` property to `'underline'`, as shown by Figure 13-5.

The Difference Between Properties in CSS and JavaScript

Something important to note here is that the `textDecoration` property is an example of a CSS property that is normally hyphenated like this: `text-decoration`. But since JavaScript reserves the hyphen character for use as a mathematical operator, whenever you access a hyphenated CSS property you must omit the hyphen and set the character immediately following it to uppercase. Another example of this is the `font-size` property (for example), which is referenced in JavaScript as `fontSize` when placed after a period operator, like this:

```
MyObject.fontSize = '16pt'
```

The only possible alternative to this is to be more long-winded and use the `setAttribute()` function, which does support (and in fact requires) standard CSS property names, like this:

```
MyObject.setAttribute('font-size', '16pt')
```

Note: *Some versions of Microsoft Internet Explorer are picky about using the JavaScript-style CSS property names under specific conditions. So if you ever encounter problems with them, simply revert to the long-form and use the* `setAttribute()` *function and you should be alright.*

Summary of the Three Functions

So now you have three powerful functions you can use for quick and easy access of any individual web document (using `O()`), it's `style` property (using `S()`), or a group of objects by class (using `C()`).

Together these will save you countless lines of programming code and speed up your development time substantially. Simply remember to copy the following into the section of any document you'll be accessing via JavaScript:

```
<script>
  function O(obj)
  {
    if (typeof obj == 'object') return obj
    else return document.getElementById(obj)
  }

  function S(obj)
```

```
  {
    return O(obj).style
  }

  function C(name)
  {
    var elements = document.getElementsByTagName('*')
    var objects  = []

    for (var i = 0 ; i < elements.length ; ++i)
      if (elements[i].className == name)
        objects.push(elements[i])

    return objects
  }
</script>
```

With this code pasted at the start of your web pages, JavaScript programming should be as easy as possible. Better still, instead of pasting them in, include the *mainfunctions.js* file supplied in the companion archive, like this:

```
<script src='mainfunctions.js'></script>
```

Just place that single line in the `<head>` of any web pages that access the functions.

Note: I use the functions `O()`, `S()`, and `C()` in the remainder of this course as they substantially reduce the examples down in size, and also make them far easier for you to follow what's going on. I therefore assume you have included these functions at the start of your document as previously discussed, and I will therefore not repeat their definitions in further examples.

Some Common Properties

Using JavaScript you can modify any property of any element in a web document, in a similar manner to using CSS. I have already shown how to access CSS properties using either the JavaScript short-form or the `setAttribute()` function to use exact CSS property names. Therefore I won't bore you by detailing all of these hundreds of properties.

Rather I'd like, to show you how to access just a few of the CSS properties as an overview of some of the things you can do.

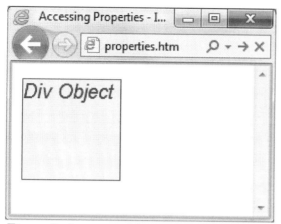

Figure 6: A <div> with various properties modified.

First, then, let's look at modifying a few CSS properties from JavaScript using the following code, which first creates a <div> object, and then statements within a <script> section of HTML modify various of its attributes:

```
<div id='object'>Div Object</div>

<script>
  S('object').border     = 'solid 1px red'
  S('object').width      = '100px'
  S('object').height     = '100px'
  S('object').background = '#eee'
  S('object').color      = 'blue'
  S('object').fontSize   = '15pt'
  S('object').fontFamily = 'Helvetica'
  S('object').fontStyle  = 'italic'
</script>
```

Remember that this assumes you have included the set of three functions I provided earlier in the <head> of the web page first. Figure 13-6 shows the result of applying this code (available as *properties.htm* in the accompanying archive).

Note: For a thorough introduction to CSS may I recommend my "CSS and CSS3 Crash Course", which is available on Amazon (in print and for Kindle), and in all good bookstores. It is also available as an on-line course (with over three hours of additional video tutorials) at the following URL:

tinyurl.com/css3course

Properties (a - l)	Sets and/or Returns
closed	Returns a Boolean value indicating whether a window has been closed or not
defaultStatus	Sets or returns the default text in the status bar of a window
document	Returns the document object for the window
frames	Returns an array of all the frames and iframes in the window
history	Returns the history object for the window
innerHeight	Sets or returns the inner height of a window's content area
innerWidth	Sets or returns the inner width of a window's content area
length	Returns the number of frames and iframes in a window
location	Returns the location object for the window

Table 13-1a: Window properties (a through l).

Other properties

JavaScript also opens up access to a very wide range of other properties too, such as the width and height of the browser, and the same for any pop-up or in-browser windows or frames, and handy information such as the parent window (if there is one), and the history of URLs visited this session.

All these properties are accessed from the window object via the period operator (for example window.name), and Tables 13-1a to 13-1c list them all, along with descriptions of each.

Properties (m - r)	Sets and/or Returns
name	Sets or returns the name of a window
navigator	Returns the navigator object for the window
opener	Returns a reference to the window that created the window
outerHeight	Sets or returns the outer height of a window, including tool and scroll bars
outerWidth	Sets or returns the outer width of a window, including tool and scroll bars
pageXOffset	Returns the pixels the document has been scrolled horizontally from the left of the windo
pageYOffset	Returns the pixels the document has been scrolled vertically from the top of the window
parent	Returns the parent window of a window

Table 13-1b: Window properties (from m through r)

Properties (s - z)	Sets and/or Returns
screen	Returns the screen object for the window
screenLeft	Returns the x coordinate of the window relative to the screen
screenTop	Returns the y coordinate of the window relative to the screen
screenX	Returns the x coordinate of the window relative to the screen
screenY	Returns the y coordinate of the window relative to the screen
self	Returns the current window
status	Sets or returns the text in the status bar of a window
top	Returns the top browser window

Table 13-1c: Window properties (from s through z).

There are a few points to note about some of these properties.

- The `defaultStatus` and `status` properties can be set only if users have modified their browsers to allow it (very unlikely).
- The `history` object cannot be read from (so you cannot see where your visitors have been surfing). However it supports the `length` property to determine how long the history is, and the `back()`, `forward()`, and `go()` methods, to navigate to specific pages in the history.
- When you need to know how much space there is available in a current window of the web browser just read the values in `window.innerHeight`, and `window.innerWidth` – I often use these values for centering in-browser pop-up alert or confirm dialog windows..
- The `screen` object supports the following read properties: `availHeight`, `availWidth`, `colorDepth`, `height`, `pixelDepth`, and `width`, and is therefore great for determining information about the user's display.

These few items of information will get you started and already provide you with many new and interesting things you can do with JavaScript. But, in fact, there are far more properties and methods available than can be covered in a crash course such as this. However, now that you know how to access and use properties, all you need is a resource listing them all, so I recommend you check out the following URL as a good initial point to start:

tinyurl.com/domproperties

Inline JavaScript

Using `<script>` tags isn't the only way you can execute JavaScript statements. You can also access JavaScript from within HTML tags, which makes for great dynamic interactivity.

For example, to add a quick effect when the mouse passes over an object you can use the following HTML, which displays one image, but replaces it with another when the mouse passes over:

```
<img src='dad.jpg'
  onmouseover="this.src='mom.jpg'"
   onmouseout="this.src='dad.jpg'" />
```

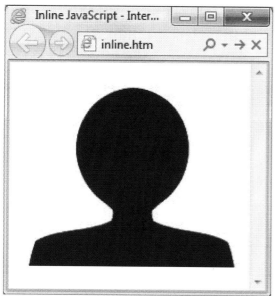

Figure 7: Applying JavaScript to HTML tag events.

Another Instance of `this`

In the preceding example you see another instance of the `this` keyword in use, where it tells the JavaScript to operate on the calling object, namely the `<img />` tag. You can see the result in Figure 13-7, created using the file *inline.htm* from the companion archive – try it for yourself and you'll see how the *mom.jpg* image swaps in an out as you pass your mouse over the *dad.jpg* image.

Non-inline Event Attaching

The preceding code is the equivalent of providing an ID to the `<img />` tag, and then attaching the actions to the tag's mouse events, like this:

```
<img id='object' src='dad.jpg' />

<script>
  O('object').onmouseover = function()
    { this.src = 'mom.jpg' }
  O('object').onmouseout = function()
    { this.src = 'dad.jpg' }
</script>
```

This code applies the `id` of `'object'` to the tag in the HTML section. Then proceeds to manipulate it separately in the JavaScript section by attaching anonymous functions to each event.

Note: Any of the preceding methods are fine for attaching to element events, and the one you use is entirely up to you. However, I would personally reserve the first style (inline JavaScript) just for popping in quick bits of interactivity here and there, and would normally use the second (separate JavaScript) when I am writing a lot of code. I do this because when programs get larger I like all the code to be in the same place where I can work on it independently from the HTML. It also separates the code from the content, so that I can easily go in and change the event actions in the JavaScript section, without touching the HTML.

Attaching to Other Events

Using either inline or separate JavaScript there are several events to which you can attach actions, providing a wealth of additional features you can provide for your users. Table 13-2 lists these events, and details when they will be triggered.

Note: You can attach to these events in either previously described manner, but make sure you attach events to objects that make sense. For example, an object that is not a form will not respond to the `onsubmit` event.

Adding New Elements

With JavaScript you are not limited to only manipulating the elements and objects supplied to a document in its HTML. In fact you can create objects at will by inserting them into the DOM.

For example, suppose you need a new `<div>` element. Here's one way you can add it to the web page:

```
newdiv = document.createElement('div')
document.body.appendChild(newdiv)
```

First the new element is created with `createElement()`, but it isn't yet inserted into the DOM and so won't be displayed. Then the `appendChild()` function is called and the element gets inserted into the DOM, and therefore is displayed.

Event	Occurs
onabort	When an image's loading is stopped before completion
onblur	When an element loses focus
onchange	When any part of a form has changed
onclick	When an object is clicked
ondblclick	When an object is double-clicked
onerror	When a JavaScript error is encountered
onfocus	When an element gets focus
onkeydown	When a key is being pressed (inc. Shift, Alt, Ctrl, and Esc)
onkeypress	When a key is being pressed (not Shift, Alt, Ctrl, and Esc)
onkeyup	When a key is released
onload	When an object has loaded
onmousedown	When the mouse button is pressed over an element
onmousemove	When the mouse is moved over an element
onmouseout	When the mouse leaves an element
onmouseover	When the mouse passes over an element from outside it
onmouseup	When the mouse button is released
onsubmit	When a form is submitted
onreset	When a form is reset
onresize	When the browser is resized
onscroll	When the document is scrolled
onselect	When some text is selected
onunload	When a document is removed

Table 2: Events and when they are triggered.

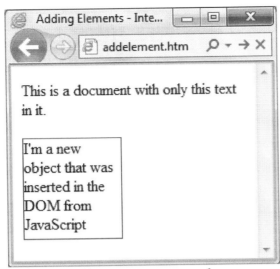

Figure 8: Adding a `<div>` to a web page.

Figure 13-8 shows this code (*addelement.htm* in the companion archive) being used to add a new `<div>` element to a web document. This new element is exactly the same as if it had been included in the original HTML, and has all the same properties and methods available.

I sometimes use this method when I want to create in-browser pop-up windows because it doesn't rely on there having to be a spare `<div>` available in the DOM.

Removing Elements

You can also remove elements from the DOM, including ones that you didn't insert using JavaScript. It's just as easy as adding an element and works like this, assuming the element to remove is in the object `element`:

```
element.parentNode.removeChild(element)
```

This code accesses the element's `parentNode` object so that it can remove the element from that node. Then it calls the `removeChild()` method on that object, passing the object to be removed.

Alternatives to Adding and Removing Elements

Inserting an element is intended for adding major new objects into a web page. But if all you intend doing is hiding and revealing objects according to an onmouseover or other event, don't forget that there are always a couple of CSS properties you can use for this purpose, without taking such drastic measures as creating and deleting DOM elements.

For example, when you want to make an element invisible but leave it in place (and with all the elements surrounding it remaining in their positions) you can simply set the object's visibility property to 'hidden', like this:

```
MyObject.visibility = 'hidden'
```

And to redisplay the object you can use the following:

```
MyObject.visibility = 'visible'
```

You can also collapse elements down to occupy zero width and height (with all objects around it filling in the freed up space) like this:

```
MyObject.display = 'none'
```

To then restore an element to its original dimensions you would use the following:

```
MyObject.display = 'block'
```

Note: While you're at it, don't forget other great CSS properties you can access from JavaScript, such as opacity for setting the visibility of an object to somewhere between visible and invisible, or simply changing the width and height properties of an object to resize it. And, of course, using the position property with values of 'absolute', 'static' or 'relative', you can even locate an object anywhere in the browser window that you like.

Summary

Having now learned numerous ways of interacting with web pages using the DOM, the things you can do with JavaScript are now limited only by your imagination. That said, I want to show you a few of the advanced things you can do before you signing you off this course. So in the final lecture I'll explain how to use cookies, make use of environment variables, write interrupt-driven code and handle Ajax communication in the background with a web server.

ADVANCED JAVASCRIPT

By following this lecture you will:

✓ *Discover how to use cookies and local storage.*

✓ *Understand how to use interrupts for animation and more .*

✓ *Learn how to perform background Ajax communication .*

YOUR JOURNEY TO become a master JavaScript programmer is almost complete, but there are just a few odd bits and pieces I still have to tell you about in this final lecture – sort of the icing on the cake of JavaScript.

These include how to save information on your user's computers to personalize their browsing experience on your web pages, how to get useful information from the browser's environment, and how to set up interrupts to provide animations and background Ajax communication with a web server – so I'll even show you a little bit of PHP (not much though, just a line or two, so don't worry).

Using Cookies

Cookies are those little snippets of data that get saved on your computer and which everyone makes such a fuss about because some companies use them to track your surfing and buying habits. However cookies are extremely useful and, in fact, invaluable for making your users' visits to your web pages as smooth and enjoyable as possible.

You see cookies are the means used by sites like Facebook and Twitter to keep you logged in, so that you can keep going back without having to continually re-enter your username and login details. And I'll now show you how easy it is for you to set and read cookies using JavaScript, so that you can provide the same functionality.

To create a cookie you simply assign it a value that contains the various details it needs to store on the user's computer. These include the cookie name, its contents, its expiry date, the domain to which it applies, the path to the server issuing it and whether it is secure or not.

This may sound complicated but look at the following (which I have split over three lines to avoid word-wrapping at unexpected characters),

```
document.cookie =
  'username=fredsmith; ' +
  'expires=Wed, 31 Dec 2014 23:59:59 UTC'
```

The cookie set by this assignment will have the name `username`, and the value `fredsmith`, and it will stay on the user's computer (unless manually removed) until midnight on New Year's Eve 2014 UTC (Universal Coordinated Time) – which is practically the same as GMT (Greenwich Mean Time), the time in London, England (without summer time, or daylight savings time).

However, it's actually a little more complicated than that because to be able to store values in cookies such as special characters and spaces they need to be run through the JavaScript `escape()` function, which turns the unusual characters into escape sequences. Plus, I haven't yet shown you how to set a cookie's path, domain and security.

Setting a Cookie

So let me provide you with a function you can use that will do all of these for you, including converting special characters to escape sequences:

```
function SetCookie(name, value, seconds,
  path, domain, secure)
{
  var date = new Date()
  date.setTime(parseInt(date.getTime() + seconds * 1000))

  var expires = seconds ? '; expires=' +
    date.toGMTString() : ''
  path   = path   ? '; path='   + path   : ''
  domain = domain ? '; domain=' + domain : ''
  secure = secure ? '; secure=' + secure : ''
  document.cookie = name + '=' + escape(value) +
    expires + path
}
```

If you use this function whenever you must set a cookie, all you need to think about is the arguments to pass to it, which are:

- `name` The cookie's name.
- `value` The cookie's value.
- `seconds` (Optional) The number of seconds until cookie expiry.
- `path` (Optional) The path to the issuing server.
- `domain` (Optional) The web domain to use.
- `secure` (Optional) If 'secure' the browser must use SSL.

The `name` and `value` arguments are quite clear, and now setting the optional expiry date is easier because you simply specify the number of `seconds` in the future before it should expire. So, for example, for a month's time it would be 60 seconds × 60 minutes × 24 hours × 30 days, which gives a value of 2592000 seconds, so just supply the number as the argument value to `seconds`.

Regarding the optional `path` argument. This should generally either be left as `''`, not supplied, or you should choose a value of `'/'` so that the cookie will apply across all directories on the server. However, if you really need to restrict it to a certain subdirectory, such as `'/login/'` then specify that instead.

The same goes for the optional `domain` argument. Generally you can leave this as `''` or not supply it and the cookie will work on the entire domain of the website (such as `'mysite.com'`). Or if you need to you can specify a subdomain of your website such as `'subdomain.mysite.com'` to restrict access to the cookie to that domain only.

Finally, if you have a secure web server running and wish to restrict cookie exchanges to use the SSL protocol, then set the optional `secure` argument to 'secure', otherwise (as is usually the case), don't pass the argument, or leave it as `''`.

Therefore, to make a call to only set a cookie's value and expiry (leaving all other settings at their default values), you might issue a simple statement such as this:

```
SetCookie('username', 'fredsmith', 2592000)
```

Reading a Cookie

To read back a cookie's value can also be a little tricky because all the cookies are stored in the single `document.cookie` string, so here's another function you can use to extract individual cookies from the string:

```
function GetCookie(name)
{
  var dc = document.cookie

  if (!dc.length) return false
  else
  {
    var start = dc.indexOf(name + '=')

    if (start == -1) return false
    else
    {
      start  += name.length + 1
      var end = dc.indexOf(';', start)
      end     = (end == -1) ? dc.length : end

      return unescape(dc.substring(start, end))
    }
  }
}
```

This function first checks whether there are any cookies, and if not it returns the value false. Then it searches for the value in name to see whether a cookie of that value exists, and returns false if not. If both tests succeed the cookie's value is read, escape sequences are returned to special characters, and the result is returned.

To read back a cookie you have saved on a user's computer you can use a statement such as this:

```
username = GetCookie('username')
```

The variable username will now either have the value false if the cookie was not found, or it will contain the cookie's value.

Deleting a Cookie

To delete a cookie I have provided one further function you can call to also save you from having to write your own (even though it's actually quite straight-forward) as follows:

```
function DeleteCookie(name)
{
  SetCookie(name, '', -360)
}
```

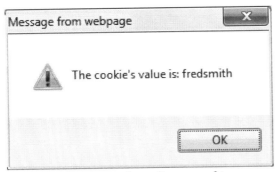

Figure 1: Setting and reading a cookie.

This function simply saves a cookie of the name in `name` with no value, and sets its expiry to -360 seconds (one hour in the past), the result of which is that the cookie expires. To delete a cookie, therefore, you use a statement such as this:

```
DeleteCookie('username')
```

These three functions are ready-saved for you in the file *cookiefunctions.js* in the accompanying archive, so that you can include them in your code as required. Figure 14-1 shows them being tested in the accompanying file *cookies.htm* (also from the companion archive), with an alert window displaying the current value of a cookie.

Once you've set a cookie for a user, the next time he or she returns to your web site just check for the existence of that cookie, and if it has a value you can use it to look up their details and personalize your content for them. You can also store passwords and other values in cookies too, and the generous 4K size limit per domain of the `document.cookie` string means you can probably store all the cookies you could want.

Note: Saving and reading cookies may not always work on a local file system on all browsers. If you intend to test these functions, to be sure they will work you need to try them out on a web server using an `http://...` address, not a `file://...` address.

Using Local Storage

If you need to store much larger amounts of data than is possible with cookies, then you can try saving them in the user's HTML5 local storage space, which supports at least 2.5MB and up to 10MB per domain, depending on the browser.

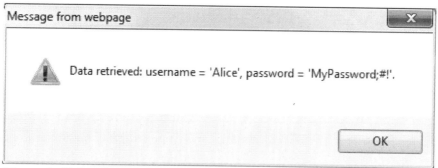

Figure 2: Values have been retrieved from local storage.

To access local storage you use methods of the `localStorage` object such as `setItem()`, `getItem()`, `removeItem()` and `clear()`. For example, to locally store a user's username and password you might use code such as this:

```
localStorage.setItem('username', 'Alice')
localStorage.setItem('password', 'MyPassword;#!')
```

If the size of the value is larger than the disk quota remaining for the storage area, an "Out of memory" exception is thrown. Otherwise, when another page loads or when the user returns to the website, these details can be retrieved to save the user entering them again, like this:

```
username = localStorage.getItem('username')
password = localStorage.getItem('password')
```

If the key doesn't exist then the `getItem()` function returns a value of `null`. You don't have to use these function names if you don't want to, and can access the `localStorage` object directly, because the two following statements are equivalent to each other:

```
localStorage.setItem('key', 'value')
localStorage['key'] = 'value'
```

And the two following statements are therefore also equivalent to each other:

```
value = localStorage.getItem('key')
value = localStorage['key']
```

Figure 14-2 shows an `alert()` message window displaying these values being retrieved from local storage, using the following code:

```
if (typeof localStorage == 'undefined')
{
  document.write("Local storage unavailable.")
}
else
{
  document.write("Local storage available.")

  localStorage.setItem('username', 'Alice')
  localStorage.setItem('password', 'MyPassword;#!')

  username = localStorage.getItem('username')
  password = localStorage.getItem('password')

  alert("Data retrieved: username = '" + username +
     "', password = '" + password + "'.")
}
```

The first part of code within the `if()` statement writes an error message to the web page if local storage is not supported in the browser. This is determined by examining the `localStorage` object and, if it is undefined, then local storage is unavailable. In the `else` part of the code a message is first written to the web page indicating that local storage is supported. Then the `username` and `password` are saved to local storage with the `setItem()` function.

Next these values are retrieved from local storage into the variables `username` and `password`. Finally an `alert()` message window is popped up which displays the retrieved values.

Until they are erased, these values will remain in the local storage once saved, and you can verify this by trying the preceding code for yourself (saved as *localstorage.htm* in the companion archive), running it once, commenting out the two lines of code that call `setItem()`, and then running it again – the alert window will still report the same vales.

Removing and Clearing Local Data

To remove an item of data from the local storage all you need to do is issue a command such as this:

```
username = localStorage.removeItem('username')
```

This serves to retrieve the item of data and place it into a variable (in this case `username`), and then deletes the data from local storage. If you don't need to first read the data you are removing, you can simply call the function on its own, like this:

```
localStorage.removeItem('username')
```

You can also completely clear the local storage for the current domain by issuing this command:

```
localStorage.clear()
```

Note: Try any of these methods on the preceding example and run it again and you'll find that the values have been erased.

The User Agent String

Every web page supplies a user agent string passed to it by well-behaved browsers. You can usually rely on this string to determine information about the user's computer and web browser. However, some browsers allow the user to modify the user agent string, and some web spiders and other 'bots' use misleading user agents, or even don't provide any user agent string.

Nevertheless, on the whole it is a very handy item of data to make use of, and takes a form such as the formidable following user agent string:

```
Mozilla/5.0 (compatible; MSIE 10.0; Windows NT 6.1; Trident/4.0; InfoPath.2; SV1;
.NET CLR 2.0.50727; WOW64)
```

Each string can be different from any other due to the way the browser is configured, its brand and version, the add-ons in it, the operating system used and so on. In the instance of the preceding string it states that the browser's Internet Explorer 10, it is broadly compatible with version 5 of Mozilla based browsers such as Firefox, the operating system is Windows 7 (NT 6.1), the layout engine is Trident, .NET framework 2.0.50727 is running on the computer, and the browser is a Windows-On-Windows program (a 32-bit application running on a 64-bit processor).

Most of these you can normally ignore, but the most useful piece of information is that the browser is Internet Explorer, because sometimes you need to tailor code to specific browsers, and most frequently that has been the case with Internet Explorer – due to a history of incorporating non-standard features.

The `GetBrowser()` Function

To extract this information from the user agent string, you can use a function such as the following, which checks a couple of other useful properties as well as `userAgent`:

```
function GetBrowser()
{
  var agent

  if        (document.all)          agent = 'IE'
  else if (window.opera)            agent = 'Opera'
  else if (NavCheck('Chrome'))      agent = 'Chrome'
  else if (NavCheck('iPod'))        agent = 'iPod'
  else if (NavCheck('iPhone'))      agent = 'iPhone'
  else if (NavCheck('iPad'))        agent = 'iPad'
  else if (NavCheck('Android'))     agent = 'Android'
  else if (NavCheck('Safari'))      agent = 'Safari'
  else if (NavCheck('Gecko'))       agent = 'Firefox'
  else                              agent = 'Unknown'

  return agent

  function NavCheck(check)
  {
    return navigator.userAgent.indexOf(check) != -1
  }
}
```

This code actually determines whether the browser is Internet Explorer by checking the `document.all` property, which exists only in IE.

Then it interrogates `window.opera` to see if the browser is Opera. After that the user agent string is tested for all major browsers such as Google Chrome, Apple Safari, Mozilla Firefox, Google Android, and various Apple iOS devices.

The command that interrogates the user agent string is the following, which uses the `indexOf()` function to find out whether the value in `check` is contained in `userAgent` (returning `true` if so):

```
return navigator.userAgent.indexOf(check) != -1
```

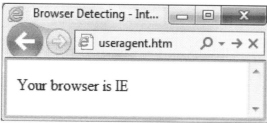

Figure 3: Returning the current browser name.

Using the Function

You can copy this function into your own code and simply make a call such as the following to assign the current browser name to the variable `Browser`:

```
Browser = GetBrowser()
```

Figure 14-3 shows this function being called using the *useragent.htm* file from the companion archive.

Note: Did you notice how the `NavCheck()` function was placed inside the `GetBrowser()` function. This is because it is called only by that function and so putting it in the function keeps the code tidy and easy to follow. However, if your code ever needs to call the `NavCheck()` function directly, then you should move it back outside again.

The Document Query String

The document query string is the part of a URL that follows the document file name and is preceded with a `?` character. Typically it is used to send Get requests from a form to a web server. A Get request is one where all the date being sent to the sever is in clear view (as a opposed to a Post request which sends the data invisibly, attaching nothing to the URL).

A typical URL with a Get request might look like the following search request made to the Google search engine:

```
http://www.google.co.uk/search?q=query+string&ie=utf-8
```

The query string here is the part after the `?`, as follows:

```
q=query+string&ie=utf-8
```

In this instance the query string has two key/value pairs (separated by an & character):

1. q = query+string
2. ie = utf8

Note: Query strings are almost always escaped so that any special characters are replaced with escape characters, and in this instance the space character has become a + character.

The GetQueryString() Function

However, it isn't only web servers that can process Get requests, because you can read query strings from JavaScript too, using a function such as this:

```
function GetQueryString()
{
  var p = window.location.search.substr(1).split('&')

  for (var i = 0 ; i < p.length ; ++i)
    p[i] = p[i].split('=')

  return p
}
```

This function accesses the query string in window.location.search. But (because the initial ? character is always included) the substr() function is called with an argument of 1, which passes on everything but the first character to the split() function:

```
var p = window.location.search.substr(1).split('&')
```

The split() function then splits the string at all occurrences of &, placing the parts into the array p[]. Then a for() loop iterates through the parts, separating each into key/value pairs by splitting them at occurrences of the = character. The string value in p[i] is then replaced with an array containing the key in its first and the value in its second element:

```
for (var i = 0 ; i < p.length ; ++i)
  p[i] = p[i].split('=')
```

Finally the p[] array is returned:

```
return p
```

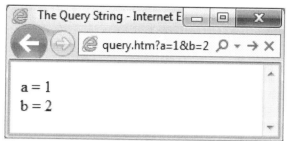

Figure 4: Reading and displaying query string values.

Using the Function

To obtain the keys and values in the query string all your code has to do is call this function as follows:

```
Query = GetQueryString()
```

The array `Query` will now contain an array of key/value pairs, with each key and value stored in a sub-array for each element. So you can iterate through the array, for example, like this (liberally whitespaced for clarity):

```
for (i = 0 ; i < Query.length ; ++i)
    document.write(Query[i][0] + ' = ' +
                   Query[i][1] + '<br />')
```

Since query strings have escaped values, when you actually want to use a key or value you will need to unescape it like this:

```
Key0 = unescape(Query[0][0])
Val0 = unescape(Query[0][1])
```

These lines assign the first key and its value to `Key0` and `Val0`, first putting them through the `unescape()` function. The second key and value (if any) could be extracted like this (and so on):

```
Key1 = unescape(Query[1][0])
Val1 = unescape(Query[1][1])
```

Figure 14-4 shows a query string of `?a=1&b=2` appended to the example file *query.htm* (from the companion archive). If you wish to test this file remember to add that string to the end of the URL in the address bar (as shown in the figure's address bar).

Note: The `unescape()` *function will not handle UTF-8 characters. So if you intend processing them, then replace* `unescape()` *with a call to* `decodeURIComponent()`, *which is a more powerful function – or better still, only use that function.*

Using Interrupts

JavaScript provides access to interrupts, a method by which you can ask the browser to call your code after a set period of time, or even to keep calling it at specified intervals.

This provides you with a means of handling background tasks such as Ajax communications (covered next), or even things like animating web elements.

To accomplish this, there are two types of interrupt, `setTimeout()` and `setInterval()`, which have accompanying `clearTimeout()` and `clearInterval()` functions for turning them off again.

Using `setTimeout()`

When you call `setTimeout()` you pass it some JavaScript code or the name of a function and the value in milliseconds representing how long to wait before the code should be executed, like this:

```
setTimeout(DoThis, 5000)
```

And your `DoThis()` function might look like this:

```
function DoThis()
{
   alert('This is your wakeup alert!')
}
```

Figure 14-5 shows this code (saved as *settimeout.htm* in the companion archive) being loaded into a browser.

Figure 5: The alert pops up after the specified delay.

In case you are wondering, you cannot simply supply the `alert()` function as a `setTimeout()` argument because the `alert()` would be executed immediately. Only when you provide a function name without argument brackets can you safely pass a function to be called later.

Passing a String

There is an exception to this, though, because you can pass a string value to the `setTimeout()` function, and then it will not be executed until the correct time, like this:

```
setTimeout("alert('Hello!')", 5000)
```

In fact you can place as many lines of JavaScript code as you like, if you place a semicolon after each statement, like this (saved as *settimeout2.htm* in the accompanying archive):

```
setTimeout("document.write('Starting'); alert('Hello!')",
5000)
```

Note: I tend to prefer using separate functions in interrupts so that I can modify the function if necessary, without having to alter the code that generates the interrupt.

Repeating Timeouts

One technique some programmers use to provide repeating interrupts with `setTimeout()` is to call the `setTimeout()` function from the code called by it, as with the following which will initiate a never ending loop of alert windows:

```
setTimeout(DoThis, 5000)

function DoThis()
{
  setTimeout(DoThis, 5000)
  alert('I am annoying!')
}
```

Now the alert will pop up every five seconds, so if you try out this code (*settimeout3.htm* in the accompanying archive) you'll need to click the Home button in your browser to snap out of the loop.

Cancelling a Timeout

Once a timeout has been set up you cannot cancel it unless you previously saved the value returned from the initial call to `setTimeout()`, like this:

```
handle = setTimeout(DoThis, 5000)
```

Armed with the value in `handle` you can now cancel the interrupt at any point up until its due time, like this:

```
clearTimeout(handle)
```

When you do this the interrupt is completely forgotten about and the code assigned to it will not get executed. The file *settimeout4.htm* in the accompanying archive illustrates this in action.

Using `setInterval()`

An easier way to set up regular interrupts is to use the `setInterval()` function. It works in just the same way, except that after popping up after the interval you specify in milliseconds, it will do so again after that interval passes, and so on forever, unless you cancel it.

Let's use this function to display a simple clock in the browser, like this (using liberal whitespace for neat layout):

```
function ShowTime(object)
{
   var date = new Date()

   object.innerHTML = date.toTimeString().substr(0,8)
}
```

Every time `ShowTime()` is called it sets the object `date` to the current date and time with a call to `Date()`:

```
var date = new Date()
```

Then the `innerHTML` property of the object passed to `ShowTime()` (namely `object`) is set to the current time in hours, minutes and seconds, as determined by a call to `toTimeString()`. This returns a string such as `09:17:12 UTC+0530`, which is then truncated to just the first eight characters with a call to the `substr()` function:

```
object.innerHTML = date.toTimeString().substr(0,8)
```

Using the Function

To use this function you first have to create an object whose `innerHTML` property will be used for displaying the time, like this HTML:

```
The time is: <span id='time'>00:00:00</span>
```

Then, from a `<script>` section of code, all you have to do is place a call to the `setInterval()` function, like this:

```
setInterval("ShowTime(O('time'))", 1000)
```

This statement assumes you have loaded in the `O()` function by including the *mainfunctions.js* file. It then passes a string to `setInterval()`, containing the following statement, which is set to execute once a second (every 1000 milliseconds):

```
ShowTime(O('time'))
```

Figure 14-6 shows this code (from *setinterval.htm* in the accompanying archive) running in a browser.

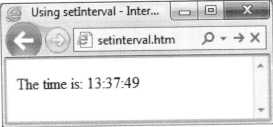

Figure 6: A simple clock created with `setInterval()`*.*

Cancelling an Interval

To stop the repeating intervals previously set up from a call to `setInterval()`, you must previously have made a note of the interval's handle, like this:

```
handle = setInterval("ShowTime(O('time'))", 1000)
```

Now you can stop the clock at any time by issuing the following call:

```
clearInterval(handle)
```

You can even set up a timer to stop the clock after a certain amount of time, like this:

```
setTimeout("clearInterval(handle)", 10000)
```

This statement will issue an interrupt in ten seconds that will clear the repeating intervals. You can try this for yourself with the file *setinterval2.htm* in the accompanying archive.

A Simple Animation

By combining a few CSS properties with a repeating interrupt, you can produce all manner of animations and effects.

For example, Figure 14-7 moves a square shape across the top of a browser, all the time ballooning up in size, before starting all over again.

The code used to produce the figure is as follows (and is saved as *animation.htm* in the accompanying archive):

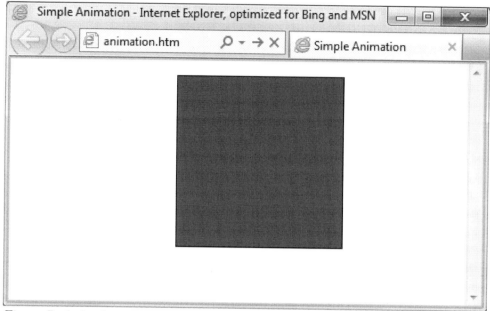

Figure 7: A simple animation.

```
<html>
  <head>
    <title>Simple Animation</title>
    <script src='mainfunctions.js'></script>
    <style>
      #box
      {
        position  :absolute;
        background:red;
        border    :1px solid black;
      }
    </style>
  </head>
  <body>
    <div id='box'></div>
    <script>
      SIZE = LEFT = 0

      setInterval(Animate, 30)

      function Animate()
      {
        SIZE += 10
```

```
        LEFT += 3

        if (SIZE == 200) SIZE = 0
        if (LEFT == 600) LEFT = 0

        S('box').width  = SIZE + 'px'
        S('box').height = SIZE + 'px'
        S('box').left   = LEFT + 'px'
      }
    </script>
  </body>
</html>
```

In the head of the document the CSS id of `box` is set to a background color of red with a one-pixel black border, and its position is set to `absolute` so that it is allowed to be moved around in the browser.

Then in the `Animate()` function, the global variables `SIZE` and `LEFT` are continuously updated and then applied to the `width`, `height`, and `left` style attributes of the `box` object (adding `'px'` after each to specify that the values are in pixels), thus animating it at a frequency of once every 30 milliseconds.

Note: I'm sure you can think of some other attributes you could animate and will have some fun playing with this example.

Using Ajax

Ajax is the power behind what came to be known as Web 2.0. It transformed the Internet because it replaced static pages that had to be posted using forms to make changes, with much simpler behind the scenes communication with a web server – so that you merely had to type on a web page for that data to get sent to the server. Likewise, Ajax-enabled sites offer assistance whenever you needed it, for example by instantly telling you whether a username you desire is available, before you submit your signup details.

The term Ajax actually stands for Asynchronous JavaScript and XML. However, nowadays it almost never uses XML because Ajax can communicate so much more than that particular markup language. For example it can transfer images and videos or other files.

Initially, writing Ajax code was considered a black art that only the most advanced programmers knew how to implement. But it's not actually the case. Ajax is relatively straight-forward as I'll show you now.

Creating an Ajax Object

The first thing you need to do in order to communicate with a web server via Ajax is to create a new object, as performed by the following function (which I showed you some of in Lecture 12 when I was explaining the `try` and `catch()` keywords):

```
function CreateAjaxObject(callback)
{
  try
  {
    var ajax = new XMLHttpRequest()
  }
  catch(e1)
  {
    try
    {
      ajax = new ActiveXObject("Msxml2.XMLHTTP")
    }
    catch(e2)
    {
      try
      {
        ajax = new ActiveXObject("Microsoft.XMLHTTP")
      }
      catch(e3)
      {
        ajax = false
      }
    }
  }

  if (ajax) ajax.onreadystatechange = function()
  {
    if (this.readyState   == 4   &&
        this.status       == 200 &&
        this.responseText != null)
      callback.call(this.responseText)
  }
  else return false

  return ajax
}
```

Let's break this down, because it's quite long but actually easy to understand. To start with the `CreateAjaxObject()` function accepts the argument `callback`, which I'll explain shortly, then a sequence of `try` and `catch()` keywords attempt to use three different methods to create a new Ajax object in `ajax`.

The reason for this is that different versions of Microsoft's Internet Explorer Browser use different methods for this, while all other browsers use yet another method. The upshot of the code is that if the browser supports Ajax (which all major modern browsers do) then a new object called `ajax` is created.

In the second part of the function there's a pair of nested `if()` statements. The outer one is entered only if the `ajax` object was created, otherwise `false` is returned to signal failure.

On success an anonymous function is attached to the `onreadystatechange` event of the `ajax` object:

```
ajax.onreadystatechange = function()
```

This event is triggered whenever anything new happens in the Ajax exchange with the server. So, by attaching to it, the code can listen in and be ready to receive any data sent to the browser by the server:

```
if (this.readyState    == 4   &&
    this.status        == 200 &&
    this.responseText != null)
  callback.call(this.responseText)
```

Here the attached function checks the `readyState` property of the `this` keyword (which represents the `ajax` object), and if it has a value of 4 then the server has sent some data. If that's the case then if `this.status` has a value of 200 then the data sent by the server was meaningful and not an error. Finally if `this.responseText` doesn't have a value of `null` then the data was not just an empty string, so the `callback.call()` method is called:

```
callback.call(this.responseText)
```

I mentioned `callback` at the start of this explanation. It is the name of a function passed to the `CreateAjaxObject()` function, so that `CreateAjaxObject()` can call `callback()` when new Ajax data is received. The `callback()` function takes the value received in `this.responseText`, which is the data returned by the web server. I'll explain what goes into the `callback()` function a little later.

The `PostAjaxRequest()` Function

You will never have to call `CreateAjaxObject()` yourself because there are two more functions to complete the Ajax process (which will do the calling of `CreateAjaxObject()` for you): one for communicating with the server by Post requests, and the other for using Get requests.

The `PostAjaxRequest()` function takes three arguments, the name of your callback function to receive data from the server, a URL with which to communicate with the server, and a string containing arguments to post to the server. It looks like this:

```
function PostAjaxRequest(callback, url, args)
{
   var contenttype = 'application/x-www-form-urlencoded'
   var ajax        = new CreateAjaxObject(callback)
   if (!ajax) return false

   ajax.open('POST', url, true)
   ajax.setRequestHeader('Content-type',   contenttype)
   ajax.setRequestHeader('Content-length', args.length)
   ajax.setRequestHeader('Connection',     'close')
   ajax.send(args)
   return true
}
```

What this function does is first set `contenttype` to a string value that enables encoded form data to be transmitted:

```
var contenttype = 'application/x-www-form-urlencoded'
```

Then either the new `ajax` object is created, or `false` is returned to indicate an error was encountered:

```
var ajax = new CreateAjaxObject(callback)
if (!ajax) return false
```

Now that an `ajax` object has been created, the following lines open the Ajax request with a call to the `open()` method of the `ajax` object, send headers to the server via a Post request, including the `contenttype` string, the length of the `args` argument, and a header ready to close the connection:

```
ajax.open('POST', url, true)
ajax.setRequestHeader('Content-type',    contenttype)
ajax.setRequestHeader('Content-length', args.length)
ajax.setRequestHeader('Connection',      'close')
```

The data is then sent, the connection is closed, and a value of `true` returned to indicate success:

```
ajax.send(args)
return true
```

The `GetAjaxRequest()` Function

The `PostAjaxRequest()` function comes with a sister function that performs exactly the same process, but it sends the data using a Get request. You need to have both functions in your toolkit because some servers you may interact with require Post requests, and some will need Get requests for their Ajax calls.

Here's what the partner `GetAjaxRequest()` function looks like:

```
function GetAjaxRequest(callback, url, args)
{
  var nocache = '&nocache=' + Math.random() * 1000000
  var ajax = new CreateAjaxObject(callback)
  if (!ajax) return false

  ajax.open('GET', url + '?' + args + nocache, true)
  ajax.send(null)
  return true
}
```

One of the main differences between this and the `PostAjaxRequest()` function is that a variable called `nocache` is created from a random number, so that a unique value can be added to the query string sent by each Get request, which will prevent any caching the server might perform by ensuring every request sent is unique:

```
var nocache = '&nocache=' + Math.random() * 1000000
```

The next couple of lines are the same as the `PostAjaxRequest()` function. They create a new `ajax` object, or return `false` if that fails:

```
var ajax = new CreateAjaxObject(callback)
if (!ajax) return false
```

Finally the Get request is made with a call to the `open()` method of the `ajax` object, the request is sent, and then `true` is returned to indicate success:

```
ajax.send(null)
return true
```

The `callback()` Function

Now we are ready to create our `callback()` function that will receive the data sent back to JavaScript via Ajax. This is another instance where the `this` keyword must be employed, as follows:

```
function callback()
{
   O('mydiv').innerHTML = this
}
```

This code assumes the `O()` function has been included in the page, and supplies the value passed to the function in `this` to the `innerHTML` property of a `<div>` with the id of `'mydiv'`. All that remains to do is create the `<div>`, like this:

```
<div id='mydiv'></div>
```

And now we are ready to call either the `PostAjaxRequest()` or the `GetAjaxRequest()` function, like this:

```
PostAjaxRequest(callback, 'ajax.php',
   'url=http://yahoo.com')
```

Or, like this:

```
GetAjaxRequest(callback, 'ajax.php',
   'url=http://yahoo.com')
```

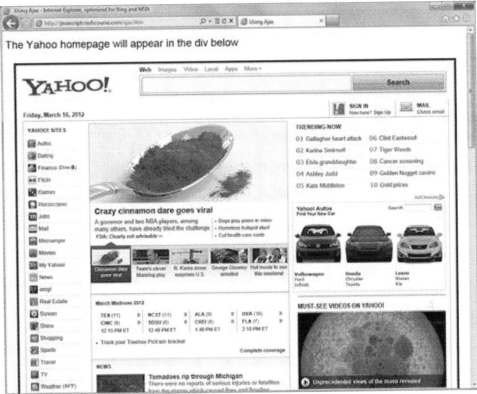

Figure 8: The Yahoo! homepage has been pulled in via Ajax.

In either instance a program in the same folder as the calling code, called ajax.php, is chosen for the communication, and the URL http://yahoo.com is sent to the program as the value of the key url.

The *ajax.php* Program

The last part of the Ajax puzzle is to write the program that will reside on the web server and communicate with the web browser. Server programs can be written in many different languages including PHP, Perl and C. But PHP is the easiest and most commonly implemented language, especially for quick tasks – in this case the PHP code is a pair of two instructions that look like this:

```php
<?php
  if (isset($_GET['url']))
    echo file_get_contents($_GET['url']);
  elseif (isset($_POST['url']))
```

```
    echo file_get_contents($_POST['url']);
?>
```

The syntax of this code is very similar to JavaScript so it's easy to follow. What it does is test whether the key `url` has been sent to it, either in a Get request (as `$_GET['url']`), or in a Post request (as `$_POST['url']`).

In either case the PHP `file_get_contents()` function is called on the value passed to it (which in this case is `http://yahoo.com`). This fetches the web page referred to, which is then returned to the calling Ajax function using the PHP `echo` keyword (which is like JavaScript's `document.write()`).

Figure 14-8 shows the result of running the previous Ajax example (saved as *ajax.htm* in the accompanying archive), which then communicates with *ajax.php* (also in the archive) on the web server, to insert the contents of the *Yahoo!* home page into a `<div>` element.

Ajax Security Restrictions

To prevent cross-browser attacks, the way Ajax is implemented is very secure. Only the server issuing a web page containing Ajax code can communicate with that page. This prevents third party servers muscling in and trying to steal your private data, or injecting unwanted advertisements, and so on. Also local file systems do not work with Ajax.

Therefore if you wish to experiment with developing Ajax code you need a web server (either local or remote) and must store your test files there, calling them up in your browser via an `http://` prefix in its address bar.

Since you may not be able to test this code on your own computer if you don't have a web server, I have uploaded *ajax.htm* and *ajax.php* to the web server hosting the website for this course. You can therefore try out the example in this section by visiting the following URL:

javascriptcrashcourse.com/ajax.htm

For ease-of-access I have saved the three Ajax functions in the file *ajaxfunctions.js* in the accompanying archive, so that you can include them in the `<head>` of a web page that will employ Ajax communication, like this:

```
<script src='ajaxfunctions.js'></script>
```

The `OnDOMLoaded()` Function

I'd like to leave you with one final function to help your JavaScript run as fast as possible, the `OnDOMLoaded()` function. If you have a web page in which you want the JavaScript to run as soon as all DOM objects are ready (and not before because unexpected results could be obtained if, for example, certain images are not yet ready), then you can wrap your main section of JavaScript in the following:

```
OnDOMReady(function()
{
  // Place all your
  // JavaScript statements
  // in this section
})

// Your functions
// can go here
```

Note: If you have ever used `window.onload` you'll find that this function will trigger far sooner due to hooking into JavaScript at the earliest point possible.

All you now need to do is ensure that the following function is alongside your code so that it can trigger your main JavaScript at the earliest possible time that everything on your web page is sure to be ready to be accessed:

```
function OnDOMReady(func)
{
  var timer = setInterval(onChange, 5)
  var ready = false

  if(document.addEventListener)
     document.addEventListener(
    "DOMContentLoaded", onChange, false)

  document.onreadystatechange = window.onload = onChange

  function onChange(e)
  {
    if(e && e.type == "DOMContentLoaded")
    {
      fireDOMReady()
    }
    else if(e && e.type == "load")
```

```
    {
      fireDOMReady()
    }
    else if(document.readyState)
    {
      if((/loaded|complete/).test(document.readyState))
      {
        fireDOMReady()
      }
      else if(!!document.documentElement.doScroll)
      {
        try
        {
          ready || document.documentElement.doScroll('left')
        }
        catch(e)
        {
          return
        }

        fireDOMReady()
      }
    }
  }


  function fireDOMReady()
  {
    if(!ready)
    {
      ready = true
      func.call()

      if(document.removeEventListener)
         document.removeEventListener(
        "DOMContentLoaded", onChange, false)

      clearInterval(timer) document.onreadystatechange =
        window.onload = timer = null
    }
  }
}
```

This code is quite complex so I won't explain how it works. But I have saved the function in the accompanying archive in the file *ondomloaded.js*, so that you can include it in the <head> of any web page that requires the fastest possible initiation, like this:

```
<script src='ondomloaded.js'></script>
```

Summary

And that, as they say, is that! You've reached the end of this crash course and I hope you found it as easy to follow as I promised at the start. You now have all the skills you need to be a proficient JavaScript programmer and are well on your way to creating popular and dynamic web sites. Before you go, though, take a browse through the appendix of JavaScript functions. I've listed most of them (omitting more obscure or technical functions) so that you'll have a handy reference to quickly see how to implement the features you need.

Thanks for taking this course, and good luck!

- Robin Nixon

LIST OF

FUNCTIONS

THIS APPENDIX LISTS the most common functions and properties in JavaScript. The list is not fully comprehensive, however, as there are still a number of complex functions and properties that are beyond the scope of this book, due to requiring advanced programming techniques.

If you are interested in seeing what they are, though, you can download the *addedbytes.com* JavaScript cheat sheet at the following URL to act as a good starting point:

tinyurl.com/jsfuncs

Arithmetic Functions

- `Number(s)` Returns string s as a number.
- `Math.abs(a)` Returns a as a positive number
- `Math.acos(a)` Returns the arc cosine of a.
- `Math.asin(a)` Returns the arc sine of a.
- `Math.atan(a)` Returns the arc tangent of a.
- `Math.atan2(a,b)` Returns the arc tangent of a / b.
- `Math.ceil(a)` Rounds up to return the integer closest to a.
- `Math.cos(a)` Returns the cosine of a.
- `Math.exp(a)` Returns the exponent of a (`Math.E` to the power a).
- `Math.floor(a)` Rounds down to return the integer closest to a.
- `Math.log(a)` Returns the log of a base e.
- `Math.max(a,b)` Returns the maximum of a and b.
- `Math.min(a,b)` Returns the minimum of a and b.
- `Math.pow(a,b)` Returns a to the power b.
- `Math.random()` Returns a random number between 0 and 0.999 (*recurring*).
- `Math.round(a)` Rounds up or down to return the integer closest to a.
- `Math.sin(a)` Returns the sine of a.
- `Math.sqrt(a)` Returns the square root of a.
- `Math.tan(a)` Returns the tangent of a.

Array Functions

- *array*`.concat(a2[,a3 ...])` Returns a new array comprising `array` joined with a2 and optionally more arrays.
- *array*`.every(c[,o])` Tests all elements of `array` using the callback function c, optionally using the object o as `this` when executing the callback.
- *array*`.filter(c[,o])` Creates a new array with all elements in `array` that pass the test implemented by the function c, optionally using the object o as `this` when executing the callback.
- *array*`.forEach(c[,o])` Calls callback function c for all elements in `array`, optionally using the object o as `this` when executing the callback.
- *array*`.indexOf(s[,i])` Returns the first element of `array` that matches s, optionally starting at element index i (otherwise starting at element 0).

- *array*.join(s) Returns a string comprising all elements in array, optionally joined to each other with the separator in string s (otherwise separated with a comma).
- *array*.lastIndexOf(s[,i]) Returns the last element of array that matches s, optionally working backwards from element index i (otherwise starting at the end and working backwards).
- *array*.map(c[,o]) Returns a new array comprising each element of array being passed to callback function c, optionally using the object o as this when executing the callback.
- *array*.pop() Pops the last element from array and returns it.
- *array*.push(e1[,e2 ...]) Pushes element e1 (and optionally additional elements) to the end of array.
- *array*.reduce(c[,i]) Returns a value determined by applying callback function c to each pair of elements in array, optionally using i as the initial argument to the first call of the callback.
- *array*.reduceRight(c[,i]) Returns a value determined by applying callback function c to each pair of elements in array working backwards from the last element, optionally using i as the initial argument to the first call of the callback.
- *array*.reverse() Returns array in reversed element order.
- *array*.shift() Removes the first element from array and returns it.
- *array*.slice(s[,e] Returns a new array comprising a selection of elements from array starting at index s and optionally ending at index e (otherwise ending at the array end).
- *array*.some(c[,o]) Tests whether at least one element of array passes the test in callback function c, optionally using the object o as this when executing the callback.
- *array*.toSource() Returns a string representing the source code of array.
- *array*.sort(f) Returns array sorted using optional function f, otherwise the array is sorted alphabetically.
- *array*.splice(i,n[,e1 ...] Returns an array extracted from array starting at index i, containing n elements from the array, and optionally adding the element e1 (or more new elements).
- *array*.toString() Returns a string representing the elements in array separated with commas.
- *array*.unshift(e1[,e2 ...] Adds e1 (and optionally more elements) to the start of array, returning the new length of the array.

Boolean Functions

- `Boolean(n)` Returns number n as a Boolean number.
- `object.toSource()` Returns a string representing the source code of object.
- `object.toString()` Returns a string of either "true" or "false" depending upon the value of `object`.
- `object.valueOf()` Returns the primitive value of `object`.

Date Functions

- `Date()` Returns a new `Date` object.
- `date.getDate()` Returns the day of the month for `date` according to local time, between 1 and 31
- `date.getDay()` Returns the day of the week for `date` according to local time, between 0 for Sunday and 6 for Saturday.
- `date.getFullYear()` Returns the year for `date` according to local time, as a four-digit number such as 2014.
- `date.getHours()` Returns the hour from `date` according to local time, between 0 and 23.
- `date.getMilliseconds()` Returns the milliseconds from `date` according to local time, between 0 and 999.
- `date.getMinutes()` Returns the minutes from `date` according to local time, between 0 and 59.
- `date.getMonth()` Returns the month from `date` according to local time, between 0 for January and 11 for December.
- `date.getSeconds()` Returns the seconds from `date` according to local time, between 0 and 59.
- `date.getTime()` Returns the time from `date` according to local time, in milliseconds since January 1st 1970 at 00:00:00.
- `date.getTimezoneOffset()` Returns the time zone offset from `date` according to local time, in the minutes in difference from Greenwich Mean Time (GMT) (can be negative, zero, or positive).
- `date.getUTCDate()` Returns the day of the month from `date` according to universal time, between 1 and 31.
- `date.getUTCDay()` Returns the day of the week from `date` according to universal time, between 0 for Sunday and 6 for Saturday.

- *date*.getUTCFullYear() Returns the year from date according to universal time, as a four-digit number such as 2014.
- *date*.getUTCHours() Returns the hour from date according to universal time, between 0 and 23.
- *date*.getUTCMilliseconds() Returns the milliseconds from date according to universal time, between 0 and 999.
- *date*.getUTCMonth() Returns the month from date according to universal time, between 0 for January and 11 for December.
- *date*.getUTCSeconds() Returns the seconds from date according to universal time, between 0 and 59.
- *date*.getYear() *(Deprecated – use getFullYear() instead)* Returns the year from date according to local time, as a four-digit number such as 2014.
- *date*.setDate(d) Sets the day of month in date according to local time, where d is between 1 and 31.
- *date*.setFullYear(y[,m[,d]]) Sets the year in date according to local time, as a four-digit number such as 2014 in y, optionally passing the month between 0 and 11 in m, and the day between 1 and 31 in d.
- *date*.setHours(h[,m[,s[,ms]]]) Sets the hour in date according to local time, between 0 and 23 in h, optionally passing the minutes between 0 and 59 in m, the seconds between 0 and 59 in s, and the milliseconds between 0 and 999 in ms.
- *date*.setMilliseconds(ms) Sets the milliseconds in date according to local time, where ms is between 0 and 999.
- *date*.setMinutes(m[,s[,ms]]) Sets the minutes in date according to local time, between 0 and 59 in m, optionally passing the seconds between 0 and 59 in s, and the milliseconds between 0 and 999 in ms.
- *date*.setMonth(m[,d]) Sets the month in date according to local time, in m between 0 for January and 11 for December, optionally passing the day between 1 and 31 in d.
- *date*.setSeconds(s[,ms]) Sets the seconds in date according to local time, between 0 and 59 in m, optionally passing the seconds in milliseconds in ms.
- *date*.setTime(t) Sets the time in date according to local time, in milliseconds since January 1st 1970 at 00:00:00 in t.
- *date*.setUTCDate(d) Sets the day of month in date according to universal time, between 1 and 31 in d.
- *date*.setUTCFullYear(y[,m[,d]]) Sets the year in date according to universal time, as a four-digit number such as 2014 in y, optionally passing the month between 0 and 11 in m, and the day between 1 and 31 in d.

- *date*.setUTCHours(h[,m[,s[,ms]]]) Sets the hour in *date* according to universal time, between 0 and 23 in h, optionally passing the minutes between 0 and 59 in m, the seconds between 0 and 59 in s, and the milliseconds between 0 and 999 in ms.

- *date*.setUTCMilliseconds(ms) Sets the milliseconds in *date* according to universal time, between 0 and 999 in ms.

- *date*.setUTCMinutes(m[,s[,ms]]) Sets the minutes in *date* according to universal time, between 0 and 59 in m, optionally passing the seconds between 0 and 59 in s, and the milliseconds between 0 and 999 in ms.

- *date*.setUTCMonth(m[,d]) Sets the month in *date* according to universal time, between 0 for January and 11 for December in m, optionally passing the day between 1 and 31 in d.

- *date*.setUTCSeconds(s[,ms]) Sets the seconds in *date* according to universal time, between 0 and 59 in s, optionally passing the milliseconds between 0 and 999 in ms.

- *date*.setYear() *(Deprecated – use setFullYear() instead)* Sets the year from *date* according to universal time, as a four-digit number such as 2014.

- *date*.toDateString() Returns the date from *date* according to local time, in human readable form.

- *date*.toGMTString() *(Deprecated – use toUTCString() instead)* Returns the date from *date* according to local time, using Internet GMT conventions.

- *date*.toLocaleDateString() Returns the date from *date* according to local time, using the operating system's locale's conventions.

- *date*.toLocaleFormat(f) Returns the date from *date* according to local time using the formatting specified in f (in the same format expected by the strftime() function in C).

- *date*.toLocaleString() Returns the date from *date* according to local time, using the operating system's locale's conventions.

- *date*.toLocaleTimeString() Returns the date from *date* according to local time, using the current locale's conventions.

- *date*.toSource() Returns a string representing the source of *date*.

- *date*.toString() Returns the date from *date*.

- *date*.toTimeString() Returns the time from *date*.

- *date*.toUTCString() Returns the date from *date* using the universal time convention.

- *date*.valueOf() Returns the primitive value of *date* as the number of milliseconds since midnight on 1st January, 1970 UTC.

DOM Functions

- *document*.createElement(t) Creates a new element with the tag name t.
- *document*.getElementsByTagName(t) Returns all elements matching the tag name in t.
- *document*.getElementById(i) Returns the DOM object of the element with the id of i.
- *document*.write(s) Writes the value(s) in s to the browser.

Global Functions

- *function*.call(a1[,a2 ...]) Calls the function function passing any number of optional arguments.
- eval(e) Returns the result of evaluating the expression in e.
- parseInt(s) Returns the string s as an integer.
- parseFloat(s) Returns the string s as a floating point number.
- isNaN(v) Returns true if the value v is not a number, otherwise returns false.
- isFinite Returns true if v is a finite, legal number, or false if it is infinite or NaN.
- decodeURI(u) Returns the URI encoded string u as an unencoded string.
- decodeURIComponent(u) Returns the URI encoded string u as an unencoded string, including any special component values such as ,, /, ?, :, @, &, =, +, $, and #.
- encodeURI(u) Returns the string u in URI encoded form.
- encodeURIComponent(u) Returns the string u in URI encoded form, including any special component values such as ,, /, ?, :, @, &, =, +, $, and #.
- escape(s) Returns s encoded by escaping special characters.
- unescape(s) Returns the escaped string s as an unescaped string.
- setInterval(c,m) Sets up repeating interrupts calling the code in c every m milliseconds – returns a handle which can be used to clear the interrupts.
- setTimeout(c,m) Sets up a single interrupt to call the code in c in m milliseconds- returns a handle which can be used to clear the interrupt.
- clearInterval(h) Clears the regular interrupts created by setInterval() using the handle in h.
- clearTimeout(h) Clears the interrupt created by setTimeout() using the handle in h.

Number Functions

- `Number(s)` Returns string s as a number.
- *number*.`constructor()` Returns the function that created this instance of number – by default this is the `Number` object.
- *number*.`toExponential(n)` Returns a string representing number in exponential notation with n representing the number of digits after the decimal point.
- *number*.`toFixed()` Formats number with n digits to the right of the decimal point.
- *number*.`toLocaleString()` Returns a string value version of number in a format that may vary according to a browser's locale settings.
- *number*.`toPrecision(n)` Returns a string representing number to the specified precision n.
- *number*.`toString(n)` Returns a string representation of number in the specified radix (base) in n.
- *number*.`valueOf()` Returns the primitive value of number.

Regular Expression Functions

- *regex*.`exec(s)` Returns an array of matches found in the string s using the regular expression regex, or returns null if no matches were made.
- *regex*.`test(s)` Tests the string s using the regular expression regex, returning true if a match is found, otherwise false.
- *regex*.`toSource()` Returns a string representing the source code of regex.
- *regex*.`toString()` Returns a string representation of regex in the form of a regular-expression literal.

String Functions

- `String(n)` Returns number n as a string.
- *string*.`charAt(n)` Returns the character in string at index n.
- *string*.`charCodeAt(n)` Returns a number indicating the Unicode value of string at index n.

- *string*.concat(s2[,s3 ...]) Concatenates string with s1 (and more strings if passed) and returns a new single string.
- *string*.indexOf(s[,i]) Returns the index in string of the search string s, optionally starting at i.
- *string*.lastIndexOf(s[,i]) Returns the index in string of the last occurrence of search string s, optionally starting at i.
- *string*.localeCompare(s) Returns a number indicating whether string comes before or after (or is the same) as s in sort order.
- *string*.match(e) Returns one or more matches (depending on whether the g modifier is used in the expression) for the regular expression e in the string string.
- *string*.replace(e,s[,m]) Finds a match between regular expression e and string string using optional modifiers in m (a string containing one or more of g, i or m).
- *string*.search(e) Returns the index of the first location of regular expression e in string string.
- *string*.slice(s[,e]) Extracts a section of string starting at index s, and optionally ending at e (otherwise ending at the string end).
- *string*.split(s[,l]) Returns an array comprising sections of string split at separator s, optionally limited to the number of occurrences specified in l.
- *string*.substr(s[,l]) Returns a section of string starting from index s, and optionally limited to the number of characters in l, otherwise all characters to the end of the string are returned.
- *string*.substring(f,t) Returns a substring of string from index f, to index t.
- *string*.toLocaleLowerCase() Returns a lower case version of string according to the current locale.
- *string*.toLocaleUpperCase() Returns an upper case version of string according to the current locale.
- *string*.toLowerCase(n) Returns a lower case version of string.
- *string*.toString() Returns a string representing string.
- *string*.toUpperCase(n) Returns an upper case version of string.
- *string*.valueOf(n) Returns the primitive value of string.

Window Functions

- `alert(v)` Pops up an alert window displaying the value(s) in `v`.
- `confirm(t)` Pops up an alert window displaying the value in `t` and supplying two options: 'OK' which returns `true` if clicked, and 'Cancel', which returns `false` if clicked.
- `window.blur` Removes focus from *window*.
- `window.close` Closes `window`.
- `window.focus` Give focus to *window*.
- `window.open(u,n[,f[,r]])` Opens a new window using the URL in `u` and giving it the name in `n`. Optionally the string `f` defines features such as height and width using a range of key/value pairs, or either `true` or `false` in `r` if the window is to replace the current value in the browser's history (ignored by some browsers).
- `window.print()` Opens a dialog for printing `window` to a printer.
- `window.scroll(x,y)` The same as `scrollTo()` (see below).
- `window.scrollBy(x,y)` Scrolls the window by `x` pixels horizontally, and `y` pixels vertically.
- `element.scrollIntoView(a)` Scrolls the element `element` into view, aligned to the window top if the optional argument `a` is `true`, otherwise aligned to the bottom.
- `window.scrollTo(x,y)` Scrolls the window to the offset from the top left of the page of `x` pixels horizontally, and `y` pixels vertically.

INDEX

29197200R00148

Made in the USA
Lexington, KY
16 January 2014